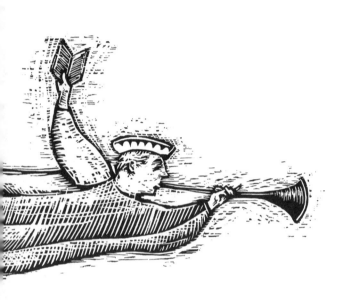

2nd Nephi: *a brief theological introduction*

This publication was made possible by generous support from the Laura F. Willes Center for Book of Mormon Studies, part of the Neal A. Maxwell Institute for Religious Scholarship at Brigham Young University.

Published by the Neal A. Maxwell Institute for Religious Scholarship, Brigham Young University, Provo, Utah. The copyright for the 2013 text of The Book of Mormon is held by The Church of Jesus Christ of Latter-day Saints, Salt Lake City, Utah; that text is quoted throughout and used by permission.

Printed in the United States of America

ISBN: 978-0-8425-0008-1

LIBRARY OF CONGRESS CONTROL NUMBER: 2019954825

2nd Nephi

a brief theological introduction

BRIGHAM YOUNG UNIVERSITY

NEAL A. MAXWELL INSTITUTE

PROVO, UTAH

Terryl Givens

The Book of Mormon: brief theological introductions series seeks Christ in scripture by combining intellectual rigor and the disciple's yearning for holiness. It answers Elder Neal A. Maxwell's call to explore the book's "divine architecture": "There is so much more in the Book of Mormon than we have yet discovered. The book's divine architecture and rich furnishings will increasingly unfold to our view, further qualifying it as '*a marvelous work and a wonder.*' (Isaiah 29:14) . . . All the rooms in this mansion need to be explored, whether by valued traditional scholars or by those at the cutting edge. Each plays a role, and one LDS scholar cannot say to the other, '*I have no need of thee.*'" [1] (1 Corinthians 12:21)

For some time, faithful scholars have explored the book's textual history, reception, historicity, literary quality, and more. This series focuses particularly on theology—the scholarly practice of exploring a scriptural text's implications and its lens on God's work in the world. Series volumes invite Latter-day Saints to discover additional dimensions of this treasured text but leave to prophets and apostles their unique role of declaring its definitive official doctrines. In this case, theology, as opposed to authoritative doctrine, relates to the original sense of the term as, literally, reasoned "God talk." The word also designates a well-developed academic field, but it is the more general sense of the term that most often applies here. By engaging each scriptural book's theology on its own terms, this series explores the spiritual and intellectual force of the ideas appearing in the Latter-day Saints' "keystone" scripture.

Series authors and editors possess specialized professional training that informs their work but, significantly, each takes Christ as theology's proper end because he is the proper end of all scripture and all reflection on it. We, too, "talk of Christ, we rejoice in Christ, we preach of Christ ... that our children may know to what source they may look for a remission of their sins" (2 Nephi 25:26). Moreover, while experts in the modern disciplines of philosophy, theology, literature, and history, series authors and editors also work explicitly within the context of personal and institutional commitments both to Christian discipleship and to the Church of Jesus Christ of Latter-day Saints. These volumes are not official Church publications but can be best understood in light of these deep commitments. And because we acknowledge that scripture demands far more than intellectual experimentation, we call readers' attention to the processes of conversion and sanctification at play on virtually every scriptural page.

Individual series authors offer unique approaches but, taken together, they model a joint invitation to readers to engage scripture in their own way. No single approach to theology or scriptural interpretation commands preeminence in these volumes. No volume pretends to be the final word on theological reflection for its part of the Book of Mormon. Varied perspectives and methodologies are evident throughout. This is intentional. In addition, though we recognize love for the Book of Mormon is a "given" for most Latter–day Saint readers, we also share the conviction that, like the gospel of Jesus Christ itself, the Book of Mormon is inexhaustible.[2] These volumes invite readers to slow down and read scripture more thoughtfully and transformatively. Elder Maxwell cautioned against reading the Book of Mormon as "hurried tourists" who scarcely venture beyond "the entry hall."[3] To that end, we dedicate this series to his apostolic conviction that there is always more to learn from the Book of Mormon and much to be gained from our faithful search for Christ in its pages.

—The Editors

Contents

Introduction
Jerusalem is Destroyed

Unique among the books of the Book of Mormon, Nephi's record is divided by its author into two books. This was not a break made by Joseph Smith or by subsequent editors. Something must have happened in the lives of the Nephite people—or in Nephi's conception of his record–keeping project—to signal for Nephi the definitive end of one phase or focus and the beginning of another. An invaluable guidepost in directing us to Nephi's motives and hopes for writing 2 Nephi would be understanding his reasoning behind the break that signals the commencement of this book in the narrative. When Nephi's people arrive in the New World, he is commanded to commence a record that becomes known as the large plates of Nephi (1 Ne. 19:1). A few decades later, the Lord directs him to begin a second record, concerned less with the "particular part of the history" of his people and more with "that which is pleasing unto God" (2 Ne. 5:30–33). This latter history, written upon the small plates, is what we read as the first few books of the Book of Mormon.

In the first book of this retrospective narrative of Nephi, we read of his ship–building project, the travails of crossing the ocean, *and* a successful landfall. Nephi's first book continues with Nephi reading from Isaiah, prophesying of the coming of Christ, and predicting a great gathering of Israel yet future. And the patriarch of the expedition, Lehi, is still alive in the story with which Nephi closes out his first book. Curiously, it is *after* his people's long journey and arrival in the promised land, *after* reading from Isaiah and prophesying about the future, yet *before* the death of Lehi that Nephi is moved to start a new book afresh. What happened, in Nephi's retelling, to signal a clear end to one stage of his people's history and the beginning of another?

We should expect an explanation in the new book's opening. And indeed, a possible justification appears just a few verses into 2 Nephi. Lehi, the "visionary man" (1 Ne. 2:11), has had another vision, he announces. And in that vision, he sees the most cataclysmic event in Israel's history up to that time. "Jerusalem is destroyed," he says (2 Ne. 1:4).

In America, as I write in the early years of the twenty–first century, men have already walked on the moon. Probes have already reached—and landed on—the red planet. Now, various agencies are contemplating a journey to Mars with human passengers. (This is not science fiction; NASA is anticipating a Martian landing in the 2030s.)[1] The daunting adventure that awaits, and that would signal a new epoch in human scientific achievement and Promethean striving alike, would be a Martian colony. Imagining a successful expedition to pioneer the technological challenges is not difficult. The next step would be a colony—perhaps a thriving outpost of civilization. An official expedition historian would chronicle their preparations, their journey of unprecedented challenge and hardship, and the foundational work of setting up stakes in a strange new wilderness. Alone and remote they might be, but they would carry with them a secure sense of mission, of origins, and of a distant though durable connection to their people back home. As colonists, they would be, in a sense, appendages of a home base, and their identity and destinies would be part of a larger narrative. What may be more difficult to imagine would be the impact of an unthinkable message transmitted across interplanetary space on such a remote and tenuous colony: Planet Earth, their home, with its teeming cities and myriad peoples, with its cultural monuments and holy places, with its childhood haunts and familiar vistas—is no more.

The comparison may not be exact, but it is apt.

For Lehi and his people, the destruction of Jerusalem changed everything. Jerusalem was the center of the Jewish universe. "No people ever placed greater importance upon their land than did the Jews," notes Jon Levenson.[2] And the temple was the center of Jerusalem. That temple was, in the words of one Jewish scholar, the "fulcrum of the universe," "the prime place of communication between transcendent and mundane reality," the inner chamber of which was "the throne room of God" himself, "the place where a mere mortal . . . can make contact with the realm of overpowering holiness, where he can hear the language of angels and respond to it."[3] No wonder that this same scholar considers that "the survival of Judaism after the destruction of its Temple and the loss of the land of Israel is the most remarkable feature of Jewish history."

At that moment, however, a future without Jerusalem and her temple may well have been inconceivable to the small band of Israelites headed into the unknown, already riven by doubts, rebellion, and factionalism. God's covenant was with Israel—but what was left of Israel? The appendage was now without a body and the colony without its home. These exiles, cousins of the family of God, now became, in very truth, founding fathers and founding mothers, inaugurating a new history from this new, definitive, point of origin. Like the moment when Cortez ordered his fleet destroyed,[4] Lehi's announcement heralded a recognition of no possible return for his small group of refugees, utter self-reliance, and an emphatically established new center of gravity. What had seemed a new chapter became an entirely new book—figuratively, but literally as well.

The rupture would have been profoundly felt, emotionally and psychologically. Indeed, Nephi's brother Jacob confirms the resulting pathos: "our lives passed away like as it were unto us a dream, we being a lonesome and solemn people, wanderers, cast out from Jerusalem, . . . in a wilderness" (Jacob 7:26). As for the Jews at Jerusalem, their response to the Babylonian captivity may tell us a great deal about Nephi's subsequent actions in constructing his own scriptural record, 2 Nephi. Scholars generally agree that the trauma of the Babylonian captivity was the principal incentive for the formation of Judaism's first canon—the Torah. As a result of "one of the most traumatic periods in Israelite history," writes one, "all of Israel's previous history and theology were called into question."[5] Another authority on the Torah writes,

> "The Priests were now facing the reality of a Jerusalem in which the First Temple was destroyed, the Tabernacle, the ark, and the cherubim had vanished. Yet sacrifices had to be offered. . . . A new Temple would have to be built, . . . and the people would have to be encouraged to return to God's ways. The surest way to do that was by offering them a holy text."[6]

Consequently, adds another, "the sacred writings became the heart of national identity. . . . Sacred writings that were almost a swan song became the means of Israel's survival."[7] This written compilation is, according to the great scholar Julius Wellhausen, what turned ancient Israel into the Jewish people by responding to "a sudden concern with the theoretical side of Israelite worship."[8] Other scholars hold that the process required "significant ideological rethinking" resulting in a "renegotiate[ed] . . . new corporate identity."[9]

So, too, with the people of Lehi. In his first book, Nephi had already given his audience an outline of covenantal history: the prophesied destruction of Jerusalem and subsequent captivity; the later appearance of a Messiah who would suffer death; Israel's scattering; and her eventual gathering, return, and conversion to Christ with the assistance of Gentiles. However, his brothers doubted such prophecies and, in any case, real-time calamity immerses us in a tragic gloom that abstract pronouncements never fully anticipate. The circumstances of Lehi's family were not those of a captive nation, but they may have felt like exiles—certainly they felt abandonment of a sort—after they learned of Jerusalem's demise. And so one can see the Book of Mormon emerging out of comparable, urgent questions of spiritual, scriptural, and historical import.

All of these questions find their common thread in the guiding, defining, animating concept of Israel's very existence: the covenant. The *Jewish Encyclopedia* notes that "the idea of the covenant of God" is traceable to "the beginning of Israel as the people of God."[10] How could Lehi's children help but ask: What, then, does the destruction of Jerusalem and her temple mean for the covenant? Have we misunderstood? Are its conditions changed? How do we now fit into covenantal history and covenantal futurity? How, exactly, do we find assurance and purpose and direction in the aftermath of this rupture? Moroni, with the hindsight of a thousand years, summarizes the project to which Nephi—as author of this new, reformulated covenantal narrative—had to now turn. Moroni introduces the Book of Mormon, which receives its thematic template from Nephi, in these words: "to show unto the remnant of the House of Israel . . . the covenants of the Lord" and assure them that "*they are not cast off forever*—And also to the convincing of Jew and Gentile that *JESUS is the CHRIST*" (title page, emphasis added).

These are the two tasks that Nephi launches in his second book, and they are provoked by a crisis without precedent in the experience of the Jewish people. He has to clarify and reaffirm to his people their place within covenantal history, after the cataclysm of Jerusalem's fall. And he must teach the full meaning of a covenant whose plain and precious parts are no longer clearly visible in the Old or New Testaments. He has to bring together the covenant's ancient roots and its future fufillment, centering and orienting that covenant around the person of Jesus Christ.

Covenant is a foundational concept in Jewish thought and identity. It undergoes dramatic revision in Christian thought and is a key to Christian theological understanding. Finally, the restored gospel is itself synonymous with what scripture calls the new and everlasting covenant (D&C 22:1). If the Book of Mormon presents us with Nephi's inspired writings on the theme of covenant, then an overview of the concept and its history is in order. Therefore, Part I will review the history of covenant theology and the ways in which the Book of Mormon works to challenge and replace the theology that prevailed at the time of its publication.

Parts II and III will then take up in turn two aspects of the covenant that Moroni heralds on the title page of the Book of Mormon. Part II will focus on the fact that, although they are a branch cut off from the main house of Israel, Lehi's people are not forgotten. Part III will then address the Book of Mormon's purpose in establishing recognition of Jesus as the Christ and as the foundation on which the covenant is predicated. Finally, Part IV will survey some of the seminal contributions 2 Nephi makes to other aspects of restoration doctrine.

PART I

The New (and Very Old) Covenant

I

The New (and Very Old) Covenant

One contemporary remembered Joseph Smith relating a crucial detail about his First Vision of 1820: according to Levi Richards, he said that on that spring morning, the Lord had confirmed to him that "all the sects" were "wrong, & that the Everlasting covenant was broken."[1] The breaking of the everlasting covenant was reaffirmed scripturally more than a decade later in the Lord's preface to the Doctrine and Covenants (1:15). It is clear from this statement, and from all that unfolds over the following years of the restoration, that the everlasting covenant is not a *part* of the gospel; it is the master framework that encompasses the entire gospel, or what Alma₂ ☞ will call "the great plan of happiness" (Alma 42:8). If Joseph Smith was told at the commencement of his life's work that Christendom had departed from the everlasting covenant, then we would expect to find that covenant reaffirmed, clarified, and restored through the "keystone of our religion,"[2] and that, in fact, is what we find. This is not simple conjecture; a revelation from the Lord actually refers to the Book of Mormon as "the new covenant" (D&C 84:57). No matter deserves greater attention on the part of those to whom the Book of Mormon has been revealed in this dispensation.

In 1 Nephi, the Lord made Nephi a crucial promise that offered some compensation, consolation, and

☞ Subscripts differentiate Alma the Elder from Alma the Younger for quick reference. Other series volumes employ subscripts to similarly distinguish other Book of Mormon figures who share the same name: Mosiah, Helaman, Nephi, and so forth.

guidance for the generations to follow: if they would keep the Lord's commandments, they would be blessed and prospered in their new abode; it would be to them a new land of promise (see 2:20–24). However, it is in 2 Nephi that Nephi undertakes the task of a more comprehensive engagement with the universal nature of God's covenantal promises and God's designs and intentions for the human family.

premortal contexts

Doubtless a spectator walking into the second act of *Hamlet* thinking it was the first would make very different sense of the action unfolding than the person who watched Act I, which set the stage for all that was to follow. As it stands, the Creation narrative of Genesis is a baffling story. The provocation in Eden seems illogical, the expulsion from Eden unanticipated, the coming of children and numerous posterity a random side effect, and the inherited burden of universal pain and so much suffering unjust collateral damage. In the Book of Abraham, and further expounded upon in Joseph Smith's well-known King Follett sermon (delivered a few months before his death), we find the background to provide a coherent rationale to those events. At some moment in a distant, primeval past, "God Himself found Himself in the midst of spirits and glory. Because He was greater, He saw proper to institute laws whereby the rest, who were less in intelligence, could have a privilege to advance like Himself and be exalted with Him." 🐟

🐟 Stan Larson, "The King Follett Discourse: A Newly Amalgamated Text," BYU *Studies* 18, no. 2 (Winter 1978): 204. In another sermon, Joseph Smith summarized the everlasting covenant as follows: "The design of God before the foundation of the world was that we should take tabernacles that through faithfulness we should over come & thereby obtain a resrection [sic] from the dead, in this wise obtain glory honor power and dominion." Andrew F. Ehat and Lyndon W. Cook, eds., *The Words of Joseph Smith* (Orem, UT: Grandin Book Company, 1991), 207.

Joseph Smith teaches that this plan involved, on Heaven's part, God the Creator, God the Redeemer, and God the Testator, who entered into "everlasting covenant . . . before the organization of this earth."[3] This Godhead made provision for the guiding powers and precepts, the formal structures and heavenly endowments necessary to shepherd us back to their presence after the educative crucible of mortal embodiment. As Joseph Smith taught, "the powers of the priesthood and the keys thereof" were designed for this end "from before the foundation of the world."[4] These provisions included the ordinances that would be employed to seal the human family into union with the divine family;[5] the related details, including the work of gathering and the construction of temples; as well as the "rules and principles" leading to a godly life.[6] In sum, God made every necessary "provision . . . from before the foundation of the world" so that "every spirit in the world can be ferreted out and saved."[7] That was the everlasting covenant outlined in heaven, subscribed to by all who enter mortality, and celebrated by "all the sons [and daughters] of God[, who] shouted for joy" (Job 38:7).

This conception of a covenant that precedes the world's existence—wherein (1) a divine Heavenly Father and Mother invite humans to acquire a divine nature and enter into an eternal relationship with them, and (2) the human family commits in turn to the terms and conditions of such an outcome—is the governing blueprint of what we call the plan of salvation, or "the great plan of happiness" in Alma$_2$'s phrasing (Alma 42:8).

Before such knowledge of premortal councils faded from human memory, an ancient poet celebrated this covenant, describing how a royal couple

> sent me on a mission
> from our home in the east. . . .

They took off my bright robe of glory, which
they had made for me out of love,
and took away my purple toga, which was
woven to fit my stature.
They made a covenant with me
and wrote it in my heart so I would not forget
(emphasis added).[8]

Only fragmentary traces of this cosmic context
remain in the biblical record. As with many features
of the restoration, such catastrophic erasures may
be examples of what Nephi referred to a dozen times
as the loss of the Bible's "plain and precious parts."
However, according to what an angel tells Nephi (in the
vision recorded in 1 Nephi 13), the consequence of the
Bible's incompleteness and denuding of gospel truths
is the "awful woundedness" of those of the future who
live outside the gospel's reach (verse 32).☞ At the
same time, the angel promised that God would rescue the "Gentiles" from this position of disadvantage,
hurt, and spiritual blindness that was not of their own
making. In the context of Nephi's words about missing
truths and their recovery, Joseph Smith's conceptions
of apostasy and restoration find very particular shades
of meaning. In premortal councils, God proposed an
eternal binding together of the human family, established laws, and instituted ordinances, along with a
mortal educative process, for the purpose of shaping us
into the kinds of beings, in the kinds of relationships,
that constitute the life of God, that is, eternal life. We
know, in fact, that the earth was created for this very
purpose: to place the human family into eternal order.

☞ "Woundedness" was the term Nephi used, according to the 1830
text of the Book of Mormon, to characterize the human condition.
Subsequent editions changed the word to "blindness," but in
either case, the blame for the condition is placed on the deficient
biblical text.

Marriage was ordained and families established "that the earth might answer the end of its creation; and that it might be filled with the measure of man, according to his creation before the world was made" (D&C 49:17). Unfortunately, through historical processes and corruptions willful and inadvertent, the larger cosmic context for this project was lost. As a result, the grand design was obscured, and fallible humans and their institutions rewrote the covenant in a tragically attenuated form of limited prehistory, extent, and impact.

The Lord revealed to Joseph Smith as early as his First Vision that the everlasting covenant had been broken. So also did the Lord make clear, in his own preface to the Doctrine and Covenants at the time of the Church's organization, that the prophet had, in fact, been called to remedy that loss: he was called as the prophetic emissary through whom "mine everlasting covenant might be established" (1:22).

the old testament covenant

In the version of the covenant God made with Israel, which has been transmitted historically through the books of the Old Testament, place is paramount. To Abraham, God makes the promise that he will lead him "unto a land that I will shew thee," there to make of him "a great nation" (Genesis 12:1–2). Subsequently, at the conclusion of a specially directed sacrifice, God seals the covenant more concretely by bestowing upon Abraham and his posterity "this land, from the river of Egypt unto the great river, the river Euphrates" (15:18–21).

According to the version of the covenant reaffirmed with Moses, which has been a mainstay of Jewish identity and faith, at least as it is recorded in the book of Deuteronomy, this inheritance and perpetual possession of the promised land are conditioned on their faithfulness:

> And it shall come to pass, if ye shall hearken diligently unto my commandments which I command you this day, to love the Lord your God, and to serve him with all your heart and with all your soul, That I will give you the rain of your land in his due season . . . . And I will send grass in thy fields for cattle, that thou mayest eat and be full . . . . That your days may be multiplied, and the days of your children, in the land which the Lord sware unto your fathers to give to them, as the days of heaven upon the earth. For if ye shall diligently keep all these commandments which I command you, to do them, to love the Lord your God, to walk in all his ways, and to cleave unto him . . . . Every place whereon the soles of your feet shall tread shall be yours: from the wilderness and Lebanon, from the river, the river Euphrates, even unto the uttermost sea shall your coast be. (Deut. 11:13–24)

Through latter–day revelation, we understand that this covenant made with Abraham not only involves blessings as well as responsibilities much greater than land and kingdoms but also applies to a much more expansive definition of Israel. In the Pearl of Great Price, God tells Abraham that his posterity "shall bear this ministry and Priesthood unto all nations; And I will bless them through thy name; for as many as receive this Gospel shall be called after thy name, and shall be accounted thy seed" (Abr. 2:9–10). In other words, this is a universal covenant insofar as it applies to the entire human family, whether Israel by inheritance or adoption. And the covenant is here explicitly predicated on the gospel, that is, on the mission of and faith in Jesus Christ. That definition is clearly taught by Paul in the New Testament. Latter–day revelation, however, reveals that these were always the terms and scope of the covenant; they were not modified in the light of Christ's advent and death on the cross.

In what sense this "Priesthood" will be borne "unto all nations" is not clear in this passage. In Joseph Smith's understanding, the priesthood associated with Abraham is temple priesthood, the priesthood of sealing and uniting the human family. In that sense, too, the keys associated with Abraham and his descendants represent the ultimate amplification of the covenant to encompass all people.

The version of the covenant we find in the Book of Abraham is lacking in the Old Testament record. And so the focus of the latter remains on the Holy Land and on the Jewish people. This covenantal understanding, with its focus on place, is crucial to understanding the effect on the Jewish people of Jerusalem's destruction announced by Lehi. Jerusalem had been the center of Israelite identity since the moment, hundreds of years earlier, when King David relocated the capital of Israel from Hebron to Jerusalem. Ever after, Jerusalem was "the Jewish Holy City," and "it would be hard to overstate the titanic trauma that the destruction of Jerusalem, and of its temple, inflicted on the Jewish psyche when the Babylonians conquered the land and city." As one Jewish scholar writes, "this holiness ceased with the destruction of the Temple and the dispersion of the Jewish people."[10] Soon after the advent of Christianity, however, a new narrative emerged that reinterpreted covenantal understanding as having two different phases and manifestations.

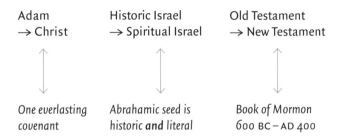

Nineteenth–Century Protestant Covenant Theology

Adam
→ Christ

Historic Israel
→ Spiritual Israel

Old Testament
→ New Testament

One everlasting covenant

Abrahamic seed is historic and literal

Book of Mormon 600 BC – AD 400

Book of Mormon Covenant Theology

christian covenant theology

The Christian tradition, historically, has not been generous to the Jewish people. The tradition developed a particular version of covenant theology called "supersessionism." According to one version, widespread for much of the past two thousand years, "because the Jews refused to receive Jesus as Messiah, they were cursed by God, [and] are no longer in covenant with God."[11] Most Christians have moved beyond supersessionism, but at the time of the Book of Mormon's publication, most Christians understood the Mosaic covenant to be a simple reiteration of the covenant made with Adam and Eve in the garden.[12] And the belief was general that in the aftermath of Adam's (and Israel's) failure to fulfill his (and their) obligation of perfect obedience, God made provision for a new covenant—the covenant of grace, inaugurated by Christ's atoning sacrifice. The New Testament was believed to articulate this new contract with God, in contrast with the Old Testament, which supposedly describes the old, original covenant. This would make the Old Testament (1) a summary of the first covenant and (2) the history of Israel's failure to fulfill that covenant. As one standard reference work

19

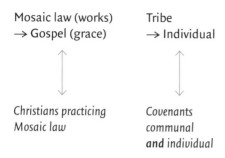

Mosaic law (works)	Tribe
→ Gospel (grace)	→ Individual
↑	↑
↓	↓
Christians practicing	*Covenants*
Mosaic law	*communal*
	and individual

FIGURE 1 Comparison of nineteenth–century covenant theology and its Book of Mormon counterpart.

explains, Protestants understand the first to be "a covenant of works with Adam, the failure of which through Adam's disobedience led to transmitted original sin." This original covenant, which ended in catastrophe, was replaced with "the covenant of grace in Jesus Christ."[13] In Catholic terms, Jesus replaces Moses as mediator of God's relationship to the world.[14] To be a Christian, in sum, has often meant to see the old covenant as displaced and superseded by the new covenant centering in Jesus Christ.

In this view, so catastrophic was Adam and Eve's failure that not only they but also their posterity suffered both spiritual death and perpetual condemnation. Many Christians invoked Israel's perceived failure to abide the terms of God's covenant with Abraham to explain their historic travails as a people and justify centuries of persecution. Christians, therefore, understood Christ to be ushering in not just a new dispensation but a covenant predicated on entirely new terms. A mainstay of Christian dogma for most of Christian history, this covenant theology emphasizes the radical divide between these two covenants (see FIGURE 1).

The very organization of the Christian Bible into the Old and New Testaments (the Greek word translated as "testament" means covenant) puts the two versions of the covenant into emphatic opposition and contrast. When Christians designated their scriptures as a "new testament (covenant)" a few centuries after Christ, it left no doubt that they saw themselves as participants in a new kind of relationship with God. The covenant was understood to be transferred from historic, literal Israel to figurative, spiritual Israel. And Christ's grace, rather than Adamic or Mosaic works, was seen as the principle by which salvation was to be secured. This explains why Protestants—who are particularly committed to this new covenant theology—have powerfully orientated to the grace–versus–works model of salvation. For them, the essence of the gospel is the *replacement* of an obedience- and works–based religion by one that emphasizes the absolute giftedness of salvation. They believe that history and scripture alike demonstrate the impossibility of our ever fulfilling the challenges of faithful obedience to the law. This belief— that personal obedience or worthiness was irrelevant to salvation—on the part of Luther, Calvin, and other Reformers opened the door to other doctrines that followed in succession. If we cannot earn or deserve salvation, then we are powerless to affect God's judgment. Therefore, it seemed reasonable to some to surmise that our free will is nonexistent or negligible and that our salvation is essentially a matter for God to determine, or predestinate, independently of our own actions.

the book of mormon and restoration covenant understanding

With this background in place, we may find a new appreciation and understanding of what the Lord meant by his early reference at the time of the First Vision to a broken everlasting covenant and his stated intention, in Doctrine and Covenants 1, that through the prophet Joseph Smith "mine everlasting covenant might be [re] established" (verses 17–22). The first major step in re-establishing that covenant was the bringing forth of the Book of Mormon.

The immersion of nineteenth-century Christians in covenant theology helps us understand how powerfully the Book of Mormon, with its focus on the everlasting covenant, would have resonated with its audience. In that era, works such as James Morgan's *Sermon on the Covenant of Grace and the Covenant of Works* (1818), Samuel Petto's *Great Mystery of the Covenant of Grace* (1820), David Russell's *Familiar Survey of the Old and New Covenants* (1824), and Thomas Boston's *View of the Covenant of Grace* (1827) were popular. The word covenant itself appears in the Book of Mormon 174 times, compared to only 30 times in the New Testament. It would seem that the Book of Mormon is clearly intended, to a large degree, to further the Lord's purposes in bringing about a restored understanding of this foundational doctrine. In fact, at one point the Lord through Joseph Smith actually referred to the Book of Mormon as the "new covenant" (D&C 84:57).

As we saw above, most Christians of Joseph Smith's day understood God to have worked throughout history by way of two very distinct covenants. The first was understood to be the covenant made with Adam—and renewed with Noah, Abraham, and Moses—that emphasized obedience to the law. The New Testament was thought to describe a new covenant that emphasized salvation by means of faith in Christ's atonement. The Old and New Testaments have been taken to represent these two distinct versions of God's covenants with humanity. Parting from this dichotomy, the Book of Mormon, beginning most emphatically with 2 Nephi, collapses these polarities into one, effectively synthesizing the old and new covenants into one everlasting covenant (hinting toward the eternal new and everlasting covenant that comprises the gospel plan laid out before the foundations of the world). And so we can see that the binaries shown in figure 1 above effectively come together.

First and most obviously, the historical setting of the Book of Mormon encompasses both Old and New Testament time frames. The narrative begins in the Old World, in the city of Jerusalem "in the reign of King Zedekiah, king of Judah" (1 Ne. 1:4). The narrator tells us Jeremiah has been cast into prison (1 Ne. 7:14), and the prophecies of Isaiah are quoted liberally. But this record chronicles an Israelite remnant's exodus under the leadership of Lehi to the Western Hemisphere and, six centuries later, describes the preaching of a New World John the Baptist figure (Samuel the Lamanite, a descendant of Lehi) on the eve of the Messiah's birth. Then, recapitulating portions of gospel narratives in this New World setting, the chroniclers describe the visit and ministry of a resurrected Christ, his ordination of and commission to twelve disciples, and the institution of church sacraments. It is as if the Book of Mormon rewrites the Old and New Testament records into a holistic gospel narrative in which Christ is the fulcrum rather than the culmination of Christian history, with both sides of the historical divide equally Christocentric.

Second, most importantly, the volume is not divided between a Mosaic dispensation and a new Christ–centered gospel. On the contrary, the preparatory old covenant of the Hebrew scriptures and the new covenant of grace from the New Testament find coexistence in the religious world described in the Book of Mormon. We read, for instance, in 2 Nephi that the ancient writers of the Book of Mormon "had a hope of [Christ's] glory many hundred years before his coming" and "[kept] the law of Moses" even as they "[looked] forward with steadfastness unto Christ" (2 Ne. 25:24). In a telescoping of the old and the new, righteous Nephites believed "in him to come as though he already was" and saw "all things which have been given of God from the beginning of the world, unto man, [as] the typifying of him" (Jarom 1:11; 2 Ne. 11:4). Faith, repentance, baptism, and reception of the Holy Ghost, with their clear New Testament parallels, are enjoined by Nephi (see 2 Ne. 31). At the same time, the Book of Mormon invokes a central image of Mosaic religion and covenant Israel—the temple—and describes its replication and dispersion in the New World. Mosaic law and Christian worship are intermingled, rather than opposed or depicted as successive versions of God's covenant.

Third, the New Testament came to be seen by the Christians of Joseph Smith's day as a work that shifted the focus from a covenantal history pertaining to a tribe to an individualized conception of covenant revolving around individual salvation. Grant Hardy notes how the Book of Mormon "portrays two distinct types of salvation working in harmony." "Nephite writers are deeply concerned with salvation history, that is, with God's intervention in the rise and fall of entire nations and peoples—Nephites and Lamanites, Jews and Gentiles—yet those same writers also repeatedly address individual sinners in need of the 'atoning blood of Christ' (e.g., Mosiah 3:18, 4:2; Alma 5:27; Hel. 5:9; Moro. 10:33)." In King Benjamin's day in particular, we see this explicit merger of personal covenant–making and communal relationality when converts pledge faithfulness to Christ but do so as a community. Benjamin's audience unitedly express their willingness "to enter into a covenant with our God to do his will, and to be obedient to his commandments in all things that he shall command us," resulting in their adoption as "the children of Christ" (Mosiah 5:5–7).

Finally, whereas the Old Testament focuses on the house of Israel as a historical entity, the New Testament moves the attention to those who are Israel by adoption (spiritual Israel). The Book of Mormon situates both peoples squarely in its view of covenant history. Nephi is at pains to emphasize, as he did in 1 Nephi 19–22 and again in 2 Nephi 9, that God's promises to Israel are intact: "they shall be gathered home to the lands of their inheritance" (2 Ne. 9:2). At the same time, Nephi weaves the latter-day Gentiles into this history yet to unfold; as the record prophesies, the Lord will "raise up a mighty nation among the Gentiles . . . upon the face of this land." Those Gentiles will bring that remnant (which "meaneth us in the days to come," notes the Book of Mormon chronicler) to a knowledge and enjoyment of the covenant made to Abraham (1 Ne. 22:6–9). In other words, the work predicts that in the modern era, converted Gentiles (spiritual Israel) will successfully evangelize the descendants of the House of Israel (historic Israel). So literal, historical Israel and spiritual Israel converge in this prophetic vision narrated by the Book of Mormon. This synthesis of literal and spiritual Israel, first indicated in 1 Nephi, is again depicted in 2 Nephi, which quotes Isaiah's vision of converted Gentiles who will carry Israel's descendants in their arms and on their shoulders (2 Ne. 6:6–7). The universalizing of the covenant is most emphatically and clearly summarized by Nephi: "For behold, I say unto you that as many of the as will repent are the covenant people of the Lord" (2 Ne. 30:2).

This may seem no great innovation since the New Testament teaches the same thing. However, the fact that this is part of Nephi's understanding makes it clear that this teaching is not a new development of the Christian era: it harks back to an earlier understanding. Some Jewish scholars note that Jewish identity is traceable to "this Abrahamitic covenant, expressive of the religious character of the descendants of Abraham as the people of YHWH, the one and only God, [and which] was renewed on Mount Sinai when, before the giving of the Law, Israel as a people pledged itself to keep His covenant."[27] Similarly, Professor of Jewish Studies Jon Levenson insists that Israel's "identity is not cosmic and primordial," or in other words, it comes out of a particular historical moment and circumstance.[28] Latter-day Saints, by contrast, believe our participation in the everlasting covenant—the participation of Jew and Gentile alike—is both cosmic *and* primordial. The covenant precedes Sinai, it precedes Abraham's journey from Ur, and it originates earlier even than God's words to Adam. It is traceable to a premortal council and envelops the entire human family. Nephi's teaching is consistent with this restoration perspective.

Another, more subtle hint toward the universalizing of the covenant appears in Joseph Smith's translation of Nephi's second book. In 1 Nephi, Jesus is consistently called "the Messiah" (twelve times). 2 Nephi 10 introduces the term *Christ*, which is employed over fifty times in this book. Of course, "Messiah" and "Christ" are both translations of an original word which means "the anointed one," and it is not clear how they would have been differentiated in Nephi's "reformed Egyptian." ☞ But the shift is significant. In his first

☞ Nephi does not indicate the language in which he writes; he used the "learning of the Jews and the language of the Egyptians," (1 Ne. 1:2) which is presumably but not definitely the "reformed Egyptian" referenced by Moroni (Morm. 9:32).

book, Nephi employs (in Joseph Smith's rendering) the transliteration of the Hebrew term *Messiah* as we would expect (since his focus is on his own (Israelite) people and their covenant history). Only in his second book— while elaborating on the covenant and its encompassing of Jew and Gentile, literal Israel and spiritual Israel alike—does Nephi switch (in Joseph Smith's rendering) to the Anglicized Greek term "Christ" that has been universally adopted by all believers. The substitution is a striking parallel to and foreshadowing of the universalizing of the covenant that Jacob teaches in 2 Nephi 10 (the Gentiles shall be blessed and "numbered among the house of Israel" – 10:18).

Related to this shift from a historical Israel to a spiritual Israel, or from the particular to the universal, is a related shift in the Book of Mormon from a geographically defined land of promise to a more expansive concept (which eventually culminates, according to Joseph Smith's revelations, in a Zion that transcends any particular place). This shift begins to unfold early in 2 Nephi, as we will now see.

PART II

They Are Not Cast Off

II

They Are Not Cast Off

As we indicated in the introduction, the impetus behind the thematic structure of 2 Nephi, if we are to judge by the event marking the narrative's commencement, is the destruction of Jerusalem. In the words that immediately follow Lehi's announcement, he offers his first in a series of consoling assurances to soften the shock of that development: "but . . . we have obtained a land of promise" (2 Ne. 1:5). A land of promise—and one of its versions in particular, Zion—has become one of the most important concepts in restoration thought and practice, as it was for the Israelites. In 2 Nephi, we find a shifting role for the concept, which provides us important ways to think about Zion. If we, as did Nephi, liken the scriptures to ourselves, then we can find great profit in studying this concept and its importance in our covenant path.

a moveable land of promise

As we have seen, the Israelites associated the covenant of their fathers with a locus in a particular place: the promised land of Israel. The intensity of Jewish love for their homeland is captured in a psalm of lament, "If I forget thee, O Jerusalem, let my right hand wither. Let my tongue cleave to the roof of my mouth, if I remember thee not; if I set not Jerusalem above my chiefest joy" (Ps. 137:1–6). Even to this day, the passionate yearning for the temple's restoration in the land of promise is expressed three times a day by the devout Jew with these words:

> "Find favor, O Lord our God, in our people Israel
> and in their prayer, and restore the Temple
> service to the innermost chamber of our House.
> May you accept Israel's burnt offerings and
> prayer with love and grace, and may the service
> of your people Israel be ever pleasing to you.
> May our eyes see your return to Zion in mercy.
> Blessed are you, O Lord, who restores your pres-
> ence to Zion!"[1]

No wonder, then, that Lehi's children would have been devastated to learn—even if they had been fore-warned—that in very fact, Jerusalem now lay waste, the temple in ruins. How many of the details Lehi beheld in his vision, we do not know. But the Jewish chronicler records that "the city was broken up and all the men of war fled. . . . And in the fifth month, on the seventh day of the month . . . Came Nebuzar–adan, captain of the guard, a servant of the king of Babylon, unto Jerusalem: And he burnt the house of the LORD, and the king's house, and all the houses of Jerusalem, and every great man's house burnt he with fire. And all the army of the Chaldees, that were with the captain of the guard, brake down the walls of Jerusalem round about" (2 Kgs. 25:4, 8–10).

No wonder, also, that in his prophetic and patriar-chal capacity, Lehi immediately acts to recalibrate his family's understanding and expectations with regard to their place in the covenant. He declares that God had reappointed to this genuine branch of Israel—his fam-ily—a new land of promise (which would soon have a temple modeled on Solomon's). And Lehi frames this assurance in language that evokes the covenant God made with Moses as reported in the Old Testament:

> "We have obtained a land of promise, a land
> which is choice above all other lands; a land
> which the Lord God hath covenanted with me
> should be a land for the inheritance of my seed.
> Yea, the Lord hath covenanted this land unto
> me, and to my children forever, and also all
> those who should be led out of other countries
> by the hand of the Lord. . . . Wherefore, I, Lehi,
> have obtained a promise, that inasmuch as
> those whom the Lord God shall bring out of
> the land of Jerusalem shall keep his command-
> ments, they shall prosper upon the face of
> this land; and they shall be kept from all other
> nations, that they may possess this land unto
> themselves. And if it so be that they shall keep
> his commandments they shall be blessed upon
> the face of this land, and there shall be none to
> molest them, nor to take away the land of their
> inheritance" (2 Ne. 1:5–9).

In other words, Lehi has affirmed the continuity of the Mosaic covenant in a New World setting. It is the fact of Jerusalem's destruction and the concern about what that means for the status of God's promises to his people—along with the people of Nephi's destiny as a now isolated remnant—that prompt the thematic thread that is so prominent in 2 Nephi (and which carries into Moroni's title page): they "are not cast off forever." Only the setting has changed.

While it is true that these New World covenant people have a new geographical setting—and it appears crucial to their covenantal continuity that, as Nephi informs us, they proceed immediately to build their

New World temple—there is also a sense in which the very principle of a holy land itself undergoes revision in the Book of Mormon. In remarkably parallel developments, the Book of Mormon systematically reconstructs the principle of a promised land even as Joseph Smith, its translator, is himself being schooled in a new understanding about promised lands.

The "promised land," or "land of promise," is an expression that appears abundantly in the Old Testament, especially the book of Deuteronomy. (The land of the "inheritance" is a related expression). Promised to Abraham by covenant, the area—roughly between "the River of Egypt" and the Euphrates River (Ex. 23:31)—became known as "the promised land" and is so referred to even today. The Book of Mormon, on the other hand, employs the term as early as Nephi's first book, but in reference to their New World place of refuge, not their inheritance in the Old World. Calling the new settlement a "promised land" (sixteen times) or a "land of promise" (twelve times) is clearly intended to establish a parallel to the Old World land of promise. The language would have served not only to indicate a covenantal possession (after all, it is God who makes that land the object of his "promise") but to suggest a kind of compensation to these refugees for their beloved land of promise that was left behind. It is no coincidence that Nephi, faithfully, and Laman, Lemuel, and Sariah, complainingly, all count the cost of leaving behind as "the land of their inheritance," the same expression used in the Old Testament for the promised land of ancient Israel (see 1 Ne. 2:4, 17:21, 5:2, etc.). ☞

☞ Some readers have posited that the term refers to Lehi's particular hereditary land; however, Nephi specifically invokes the phrase as the more general land of promise, believing Israel will be "restored in the flesh . . . unto the lands of their inheritance" (2 Ne. 10:7).

It is therefore difficult to know how Nephi's faithful followers would have responded when, after the trauma of exile and loss and resettlement in a new "land of promise," a new land of "inheritance," they suddenly become exiles again in 2 Nephi. Journeying for years in the Old World wilderness, braving a treacherous sea crossing, and establishing themselves in their new promised land and place of refuge, they almost immediately find themselves refugees again, fleeing from their rightful inheritance. Threatened by brothers who "did seek to take away [his] life," Nephi, with what must have been a traumatic sense of déjà vu, once again takes his "journey into the wilderness for the space of many days" (2 Ne. 5:4–7). In fact, one devastating loss (Lehi's death) is quickly followed by a second (renewed exile) in the very same chapter where Lehi shares his catastrophic vision:

> "And it came to pass that the Lord did warn me, that I, Nephi, should depart from them and flee into the wilderness, and all those who would go with me. Wherefore, it came to pass . . . we did take our tents and whatsoever things were possible for us, and did journey in the wilderness" (verses 5–7).

It is after this second exile from what they had thought to be their new land of inheritance that Nephi directs the building of a temple in what is now their third land of settlement (verse 16). Does the building of the temple suggest something significant about how a land of promise becomes marked as such? In any case, it would seem that with prophetic leadership, a new place of refuge, and now a temple, the Nephites' shadow of the original land of promise in Jerusalem has at this stage become its effectual replacement.

And yet, this third site, settled as a land of promise, proves to be as unstable as the past versions.

The pattern of guided exile initiated in Ur by Father Abraham, repeated by Lehi at the record's commencement, and replayed by Nephi in the aftermath of his father's death, occurs yet again a few generations later:

> "I am Amaleki, the son of Abinadom. Behold,
> I will speak unto you somewhat concerning
> Mosiah, who . . . being warned of the Lord that
> he should flee out of the land of Nephi, and as
> many as would hearken unto the voice of the
> Lord should also depart out of the land with
> him, into the wilderness—And it came to pass
> that he did according as the Lord had com-
> manded him. And they departed out of the land
> into the wilderness, as many as would hearken
> unto the voice of the Lord" (Omni 1:12–13).

latter–day parallels

One wonders if, a few years after translating the Book of Mormon, Joseph Smith and the first generation of Latter–day Saints likened this pattern unto themselves. Did they see themselves in this same cycle of displacement and disappointed hopes? Battered and bruised by dissension from within and persecution from without, Joseph Smith and the Saints were buoyed by their exuberant optimism that God had identified the land of Zion. Joseph Smith had arrived in the Missouri wilderness in summer 1831, learning by revelation that this was indeed "the land which [God] appointed and consecrated for the gathering of the saints, . . . the land of promise and the place for the city of Zion" (D&C 57:1–2). This was the place where the city of Enoch would descend to meet its earthly counterpart. All the signs were propitious for the Lord's return, and now the holy city of prophecy, modeled on Enoch's community, was within reach. On August 2, 1831, Sidney Rigdon dedicated the land of Jackson County to the Lord for the gathering of the Saints. Then the leadership ceremoniously laid the foundations for a schoolhouse. Twelve men, representing the twelve tribes of Israel, placed the first log in the first building of "Zion." The next day, Joseph Smith dedicated a site for a temple. The millennial dream was unfolding. Brigham Young later recalled those days as a glimpse into paradise: "A great many people imbibed the same idea which I did in the beginning, and really believed that in Jackson County all the earthly sorrows, afflictions, disappointments, and weaknesses pertaining to the flesh would be at an end, and that every one would be sanctified before the Lord, and all would be peace and joy from morning until evening, and from year to year, until the Savior should come."[2]

Two years later, the illusion was shattered by violent mobs and militia. Expulsion on the verge of realization from what the Saints had believed was their millennial dream was the most shattering episode in Latter-day Saint history. "The idea of being driven away from the land of Zion pained their very souls, and they desired of God, by earnest prayer, to return with songs of everlasting joy, as said Isaiah, the prophet," reported leaders Lyman Wight and Parley Pratt to Joseph Smith.[3] Their crushing disappointment was repeated again with their expulsions from Clay County in 1833, from the entire state of Missouri in 1838, and then from Nauvoo—and in effect from the United States—in 1846. By this time, however, Joseph Smith had learned that while Zion may have a place on a map and an actual plat, the more essential meaning was "the pure in heart." And that would seem to be one crucial lesson for which the Book of Mormon provided a template. Pervading Nephi's teachings on covenant and his people's sojourn from one gathering place to another is the same principle the Latter-day Saints gradually absorbed: as taught in

2 Nephi, Christ's people are "as many as will believe on his name" (25:14).

One of the most concrete articulations of the covenant God makes with Israel is found in Exodus: "If ye will obey my voice indeed, and keep my covenant, ye shall be a peculiar treasure unto me above all people. . . . And ye shall be unto me a kingdom of priests, and an holy nation" (Ex. 19:5–6). As Joseph Smith refined his own understanding of building up Zion, he mirrors the key idea from that original covenant, using language that privileges the holiness of the people over the holiness of place: "He [God] [is] going to make of this society a kingdom of priests—as in Enoch's day."[4] He saw the forging of this godly, covenant community as his true prophetic task.

from promised land to zion

Nephi's double exile gives particular force to this lesson: Zion is not dependent on place. True, Zion–building and gathering have an important place in the lives of covenant peoples. As Joseph Smith taught, education is an important reason for gathering together: "Intelligence is the great object of our holy religion." He continued, "and intelligence is the result of education, and education can only be obtained by living in compact society. . . . One of the principle objects, then, of our coming together, is to obtain the advantages of education and in order to do this, compact society is absolutely necessary."[5] The second principal reason for gathering is to consolidate the resources necessary for the building of temples. As Joseph Smith would later teach, the object of gathering was precisely this, "to build unto the Lord an house whereby he could reveal unto his people the ordinances of his temple."[6]

Zion as a "compact society" schools and prepares the Saints for the more durable construction of Zion as a people. That seems to be the point in both 2 Nephi and in the history of the Saints. Still, Nephi's own experience affirms that gathering and lands of promise fade in relative significance compared to the imperative to live as covenant people. The Book of Mormon may be seen in this light as the story of volatile and fragile lands of refuge, a testament of the portability and ceaseless transmutations of Zion, with the only constant being the eternally present promise of a personal relationship to God and direct access to his power and truth. Lehi's original dislocation and exodus become a prelude not to a new geographical gathering but a shadow of the permanent reconstitution of Zion into spiritual refuge. For nineteenth-century readers whose ancestors had embarked on their own errand into the wilderness, the resonance of this theme would have been unmistakable. And the theme would undoubtedly have held special poignancy for the first readers of the Book of Mormon, nineteenth-century religious refugees who persisted doggedly and tragically in attempts to realize their own earthly Zions in a trail that often led from Manchester, England, or Odense, Denmark, to Kirtland, Ohio, or Missouri, Illinois, and the Great Basin of Utah.

The lesson was explicitly affirmed in a revelation to Joseph Smith, when Zion was scripturally defined not as the Jerusalem hilltop it was anciently, nor the land of Missouri the Saints expected to inherit, but as "the pure in heart" (D&C 97:21). The Book of Mormon implicitly, and Nephi more explicitly, make the same point. In the very moment that his people are required to abandon this new land of promise, Nephi outlines a path—a covenant path—to assure that they remain in blessed relation to their God independent of place. It is the same covenant path that Latter-day Saints follow today. Launching their journey "into the wilderness"

(2 Ne. 5:5), they take their scriptures ("the records which were engraven upon the plates of brass," verse 12), build a temple ("like unto the temple of Solomon," verse 16), organize the priesthood ("I . . . did consecrate . . . priests and teachers," verse 26), and live the gospel ("we did observe to keep the judgments, and the statutes, and the commandments of the Lord in all things," verse 10). Nephi concludes his brief account of community building by definitively replacing the focus on a promised place with an aspiration to become a promised people. Irony drives the point home: the unrighteous who remained in the original Lehite land of promise "were cut off from [God's] presence" (verse 20). Those in the wilderness who kept the covenant path suffer no such loss and, in fact, live "after the manner of happiness" (verse 27).

So two principles of their covenantal understanding unfold simultaneously to shape and edify the people of Nephi. First, they learn that God can make any land a land of promise, a holy land. They have lived this principle, and their descendants will continue to experience its reality. Second, they learn that very real, prophetic promises tied to their place in God's designs for the human family are still intact despite their separation from the lands—and kindred—of their original roots in Israel. It is to these promises and assurances from Isaiah that Nephi devotes so much of his attention in the rest of the second book.

Much of 2 Nephi reinforces these twin promises. It is imperative to remember that Nephi is deliberately reading Isaiah so as to make him relevant; "I will liken his words unto my people," he explains (2 Ne. 11:2). He does not claim that Isaiah had the Nephites in mind but rather that the prophet's words can be adapted to his time and place in history. In Nephi's inspired appropriation of Isaiah to his people's particular circumstances,

Israel is not forgotten, and the promised land will again be theirs. And in the interim, one's place in the covenant is assured if one keeps to the covenant path, regardless of geography. Many of the extensive quotations from Isaiah (composing almost half of the entire second book of Nephi) are to reinforce the first point. They may be difficult to navigate for a modern audience, but Nephi's audience had just learned that their temple and city of promise had been destroyed. They would have needed to know, above all else, that they had not been abandoned by God and that their people would be brought back into God's fold. According to Nephi, Isaiah's words affirm "the restoration of the . . . house of Israel," "no more [to] be confounded" or "scattered" (1 Ne. 15:20). For us, greatly removed from Nephite history and culture, the lesson is that God's promises are unbreakable—and that as modern inheritors of the promises made to Abraham (after all, we who "repent are the covenant people of the Lord" – 2 Ne. 30:2), we, too, are a part of covenantal history.

Second Nephi 6 (cf. Isaiah 49) immediately draws modern readers personally into this ongoing saga. Gentiles of the modern church are, by Nephi's likening, promised to be those among whom God has "set up his standard to the people;" we have a role to play in assembling modern Israel (literally or figuratively), bringing Israel's "sons in [our] arms, and [her] daughters . . . upon [our] shoulders," which we saw above (verses 6–7). In the next chapter (cf. Isaiah 50), the Lord poses a rhetorical question to Israel with particular applicability to Lehi's children, "have I cast thee off forever?" (7:1). Chapter 8 (cf. Isaiah 51) promises that "the captive exile" will be "loosed" (verse 14). In chapter 9, in case Nephi's people (or we) miss the point, Nephi reminds readers that he is sharing these Isaiah passages "that [we] might know"—and be reassured—"concerning the covenants of the Lord that he has covenanted with *all* the house of Israel" (verse 1, emphasis added). In chapter 10, which concludes five chapters of Jacob's explanations of Isaiah, sweeping promises are extended to the latter–day gentiles: "the Gentiles shall be blessed upon the land," they will suffer neither oppression nor kings, and "the Gentiles shall be blessed and numbered among the house of Israel (2 Ne. 10:10; 2 Ne. 10:18).

Similar themes follow in the thirteen–chapter–long quotation of Isaiah that follows. Chapter 12 (cf. Isaiah 2) depicts the restoration of Israel to their rightful place of prominence in God's plans ("the word of the Lord" shall again be heard coming "from Jerusalem" – 2 Ne. 12:3). Zion's redemption, when God will again bear witness of his proximity by means of the cloud by day and "a flaming fire by night," is promised in chapter 14 (verse 5). In chapter 15, where Nephi quotes Isaiah 5, Latter-day Saints find one of the most explicit of the many prophecies guaranteeing Israel's restoration, when they "shall come with speed swiftly" (verse 26)—and so on. Chapter after chapter, God's designs for the human family unfold amidst assurances that the everlasting covenant is unbreakable. Latter–day temples will appear, Israelites and Gentiles will share in the covenant's promises jointly. Most importantly for Nephi, the promised Redeemer of Israel will come, first as an innocent and willing sacrifice for his people, then again in glory as Prince of Peace when at history's end, "the whole earth is at rest" (2 Ne. 24:7). Contemporary biblical scholarship may dispute the extent to which Isaiah's prophecies are Messianic; however, Nephi explicitly invokes Isaiah because "he verily saw my Redeemer" and "my soul delighteth in proving unto my people the truth of the coming of Christ" (2 Ne. 11:2, 4).

Only eternal perspective can alleviate the wounds of present pain and bewilderment. Nephi's inspired strategy for conveying the Lord's blueprint for covenantal history to Lehi's posterity—who were few, fragile, and twice exiled from home—was to quote from the writings of Isaiah so that, as Moroni noted, they might "know the covenants of the Lord, and that they are not cast off forever" (title page).[4]

PART III

To the Convincing of Jew and Gentile that Jesus is the Christ

III

To the Convincing of Jew and Gentile that Jesus is the Christ

Convincing his brethren and posterity that they were "not cast off," even though they must have at times felt that way, was one of Nephi's most important self–avowed tasks—and one mentioned by Moroni on his title page for the Book of Mormon. The second purpose Moroni describes on the same title page is also the second focus of Nephi's record: his testament etched on metal over twenty–five centuries ago that the man known to history as Jesus of Nazareth was in reality the promised Messiah. These two purposes appear in what many readers of Joseph Smith's day and our own consider to be a curious juxtaposition: a reaffirmation of Old Testament assurances about Israel's restoration and a testimony of Jesus Christ borne many centuries before his birth. Only when one recalls the eternal nature of the everlasting covenant do these two propositions not only coexist logically but they become indissolubly connected. From restoration teachings, we know that from its presentation in those earliest heavenly councils, the everlasting covenant depended upon and centered around the grace–drenched offer of Jesus Christ to be the Atoning One, our healer and guarantor of life eternal.

What is so remarkable about Joseph Smith as the prophet of the restoration is that he comes so early to a conception that is so radical. Mere days after the

Church is organized, before he has translated Enoch's reference to a preexistence and five years before producing Abraham's account of the heavenly council, he already refers in a revelation to "the new and everlasting covenant, even that which was *from the beginning*" (D&C 22:1). This was the meaning of Parley Pratt's later insistence that "we have only the old thing. It was old in Adams day it was old in Mormons day & hid up in the earth & it was old in 1830 when we first began to preach it."[1] The Book of Moses pushed the everlasting covenant back from the New Testament to the angel's instruction to Adam and Eve in the Garden. As *Lectures on Faith* states, "the plan of redemption [was] revealed to man," and "from this we can see that the whole human family, in the early age of their existence, in all their different branches, had this knowledge."[2]

A few years later, the Book of Abraham traced the covenant back to premortal councils. From the perspective of an eternal plan of happiness—one that was outlined in premortal realms, taught to Adam and Eve, and inherited by a faithful remnant of Israel in the New World—we would expect Jesus Christ to assume his role of absolute centrality in the covenant. From the perspective of Christian history, however, an ancient Israelite writing clearly of the coming of Jesus Christ would be illogical, nonsensical. Was this truth, too, one of the "plain and precious things" stripped from the biblical record? Nephi certainly understands the focus of his prophetic commission in this regard. As he says, in words that Moroni will quote as the Book of Mormon's second purpose: both "the Jews" and "the Gentiles [must] be convinced also that Jesus is the Christ, the Eternal God" (2 Ne. 26:12). Compare Moroni's phrasing: "to the convincing of the Jew and the Gentile that Jesus is the Christ, the Eternal God" (the title page of the Book of Mormon). Nephi understands—and assumes the burden of convincing his people—that the God whom Israel worships, the God of the covenant, the one whom Isaiah names "the Holy One of Israel," is Jesus Christ. He also understands that recognizing Jesus Christ as their God, receiving him, abiding his law, adoring him now as Jehovah, and embracing him as the incarnate Messiah to come is the purpose for which the covenant was given and the conditions by which Israel honors and abides that covenant.

This is why, in one of the most revolutionary lines in the Book of Mormon, we find the addendum that Lehi gives to his teachings on the covenant. After pronouncing the promises of the Lord pertaining to this new land of promise, as quoted above, Lehi adds this conditional:

> "if the day shall come that they will reject
> the *Holy One of Israel, the true Messiah, their*
> *Redeemer and their God,* . . . he will take away
> from them the lands of their possessions, and
> he will cause them to be scattered and smitten"
> (2 Ne. 1:11, emphasis added).

Again, the placement of this statement is important. The twin themes Moroni has previewed in his title page are here made the focus of and the occasion for the project Nephi undertakes in his second book. Second Nephi has just opened with the destruction of Jerusalem. And Lehi's immediate comfort, tied to an admonition, is that the place where they are can be their promised land, and they are still partakers of the covenant, *if* they do not reject that person who is the author and focus of their covenantal life: the Holy One of Israel, the "true Messiah," who is their Redeemer and their God. Identifying this Messiah and Redeemer as the Jesus Christ who is to come constitutes Nephi's other focus, as we will now see.

How did a group of ancient Israelites a continent away from Jerusalem and six centuries before his coming acquire exact foreknowledge of Jesus when their Jewish contemporaries had, at best, vaguely defined beliefs in some kind of future Messiah? More specifically, how could Nephi, writing in his second book, testify that "I glory in my Jesus, for he hath redeemed my soul from hell" (2 Ne. 33:6)? We know there are many early references to Christ that did not survive in the Hebrew Bible. Two second–century Christian authorities, Justin Martyr and Irenaeus, as well as the medieval *Book of the Bee* and 4 Baruch, cite currently unknown passages from Jeremiah that predict details of the Messiah's birth, ministry, and resurrection.[3] Eusebius, regarded as the father of church history, argues that "Moses . . . was enabled by the Holy Spirit to foresee quite plainly the title Jesus (evident, he believes, in his naming his successor Joshua—which transliterates as Jesus).[4] In addition, some claim that a number of Dead Sea Scrolls reveal that "at least some Jews of that time expected a Messiah who would be a divine savior, performing many miracles, and bringing the resurrection."[5] More controversially, Margaret Barker uses biblical and extra-biblical sources to argue that Christ's New Testament titles, "Son of God, Lord and Messiah," were not the result of "creative theologizing" of the first Christians, but were already present "in the expectations and traditions of first–century Palestine." They simply "fitted Jesus into an existing pattern of belief."[6] The author of Hebrews went so far as to suggest that the gospel "was first preached" to the children of Israel; Peter claimed that "all" the prophets testified "that Christ should suffer," uncertain only "what, or what manner of time the Spirit of Christ which was in them did signify, when it testified beforehand the sufferings of Christ" (Heb. 4:6;

Acts 3:18; 1 Pet. 1:10–11). As Daniel Boyarin summarizes, "versions of this narrative, the Son of Man story (the story that is later named Christology), were widespread among the Jews before the advent of Jesus; Jesus entered into a role that existed prior to his birth, and this is why so many Jews were prepared to accept him as the Christ, as the Messiah, Son of Man."[7] Shirley Lucas is another scholar who argues that far more than a vague "pre-messianism" was present among the Jewish people; a "trove," a "wealth of messianic material in the Hebrew scriptures," has long been ignored.[8] Nephi is emphatic and unambiguous about his—and his people's—knowledge of the Christ. His knowledge came to him through several prophetic figures now lost to the canon: he quotes from Zenock, Neum, and Zenos to attest to Christ's crucifixion and resurrection (1 Ne. 19:10). As a consequence of the teachings he had access to, he can say that "we talk of Christ, we rejoice in Christ, we preach of Christ, [and] we prophesy of Christ" (2 Ne. 25:26).

knowing of *Christ, and knowing Christ*

What more did Nephi in particular—this Israelite born more than six centuries before Christ—know about the coming Messiah? In the book of 2 Nephi, we hear personal testimonies of three prophets who have more than just scriptural knowledge of the promised Messiah; each one has had a personal encounter with the Redeemer. Nephi's father had had a vision in Jerusalem in which he was given a book that "manifested plainly of the coming of a Messiah" (1 Ne. 1:9, 19). Later, Lehi preaches the time of the Messiah's coming apparently based on an elaborate dream (1 Ne. 10:2–4). But it is in 2 Nephi that he bears personal witness. "I have beheld his glory," he tells his children, "and I am encircled about eternally in the arms of his love." That this God whom he has personally encountered is also the very Redeemer is a truth that Lehi explicitly attests to: he "hath redeemed my soul from hell" (2 Ne. 1:15).

Nephi's brother Jacob spends several chapters in Nephi's second book expounding on his testimony of the coming Christ: "for it behooveth the great Creator that he suffereth himself to become subject to man in the flesh, and die for all men" (2 Ne. 9:5). However, like Lehi, his knowledge of Christ is actually centered in his personal witness of the premortal Christ. As if compensating for Jacob's modesty, it falls to Nephi to add a postscript to Jacob's sermon on the Savior, informing us that "my brother, Jacob, . . . has seen him," after which Nephi adds, "As I have seen him" (2 Ne. 11:3). He has already told us, with poignant detail, that his "eyes have beheld great things," and the Lord has "filled me with his love, even to the consuming of my flesh" (2 Ne. 4:25, 21). So the first three prophetic figures of the Book of Mormon, Lehi, Nephi, and Jacob, all attest to the coming Messiah, identifying him as Jesus Christ. And each one's testimony is rooted in a personal appearance of the Christ to them, even as he appeared to Isaiah, Nephi tells us (2 Ne. 11:2).

This, in fact, becomes a motif of incalculable significance in the Book of Mormon. If this sacred record were no more than inspired fiction, then the testimonies of its mythical figures would be no more than a literary charade. The power and efficacy of the book and the testimonies it conveys are mutually dependent. Any book loosely related to the Christian tradition can adapt its themes and doctrines. Here, however, we encounter first-hand testimonials that the Christ of scripture is a living God, manifesting himself to flesh and blood individuals, reshaping our own reality as one still pregnant with possibilities of our first-hand communion with the divine. Once alerted to this theme—and to the animating power of personal encounters with the Christ (which we will see again with Enos and the brother of Jared)—we learn that the definition of prophet as given by John the Revelator applies to the pre-Christian world as well as his own age: "the testimony of Jesus is the spirit of prophecy" (Rev. 19:10).

These multiple first-person accounts shatter the historical uniqueness, and remoteness, of the Jesus depicted in the New Testament. Simon Montefiori writes that one hundred patients a year are admitted to Jerusalem's mental hospitals, suffering from the "Jerusalem syndrome," a psychiatric collapse brought on by the crushing disappointment of Christian seekers who do not find that a visit to the place where Jesus walked fulfills their deepest spiritual yearnings and fantasies. ☞ The city is replete with vestigial remnants of a presence no longer fully realized. Pilgrims desperate to capture a tangible trace of Christ's reality seek the place of his birth, his baptism, or his burial. Europe as well overflows with countless memorials, shrines, and alleged mementos of a past that persists materially into the present: pieces of the cross, the crown of thorns, or a burial shroud. But by their shriveled antiquity, such relics only emphasize the vast distance that separates us from the vanished moments of his living, breathing, bodily reality.

Into this immense historical vacuum strewn only with dusty fragments and well-worn stony paths, the Book of Mormon bursts with a remarkable, audacious claim: Jesus was not a once-in-eternity incarnation of

☞ "Jerusalem has a way of disappointing and tormenting both conquerors and visitors. The contrast between real and heavenly cities is so excruciating that a hundred patients a year are committed to the city's asylum, suffering from the Jerusalem Syndrome, a madness of anticipation, disappointment and delusion." Simon Sebag Montefiore, *Jerusalem, The Biography* (New York: Alfred A. Knopf, 2011), xxv.

the Divine, flashing like a shooting star into the long night of history. His Palestinian birth and ministry were not the beginning and end of his human interaction, and the Old World and its people are not the only setting in which he loved and healed. The Book of Mormon multiplies the field of Christ's operations and its perseverance across place and time.

As if they are aware of the improbable nature of their knowledge, Book of Mormon authors always attribute their witness to special revelations. For instance, Nephi refers to the coming Messiah as Jesus Christ "according to . . . the word of the angel of God" (2 Ne. 25:19). Jacob knows of Christ's scourging and crucifixion because of "the words of the angel who spake it unto me" (2 Ne. 6:9). The name of Christ's mother, Mary, was likewise made known to King Benjamin "by an angel from God" (Mosiah 3:2–8). The high priest Alma the Younger knows the Savior shall be born of Mary in Jerusalem because "the spirit hath said this much unto me" (Alma 7:9), and so on. Of course, this pattern does not merely account for what would otherwise be a historical anomaly, that is, Israelites with a knowledge of Christ more specific, more detailed, than any biblical or extrabiblical accounts of which we have record. More significantly, the pattern is one we are personally invited to replicate. As Nephi learned in his first book, revelation and visions and personal spiritual manifestations pertaining to Christ are not limited to prophets and patriarchs, but to "all those who diligently seek him, as well in times of old as in the time that he should manifest himself unto the children of men" (1 Ne. 10:17). When the great American poet John Greenleaf Whittier was asked how one could account for the thriving success of the Church of Jesus Christ in its initial era, he pointed to that very promise of personal revelation: the new faith, he says, "spoke a language of hope and promise to weak, weary hearts, tossed and troubled, who have wandered from sect to sect, seeking in vain for the primal manifestations of the divine power."[9] The Book of Mormon both witnesses to the ever–present possibility of such divine manifestations and invites readers to experience their own.

So, too, does this pattern of prophetic witness invite us to similarly transform doctrinal assent into animating encounter. We are encouraged to find our personal place in a universal covenant, aspiring to that moment when we, too, can say, "I have beheld his glory, and I am encircled about continually in the arms of his love" (2 Ne. 1:15). These words of Lehi are, in fact, echoed in the founding moment of the restoration, when a young Christian seeker found that he, too, could affirm that

"the Lord heard my cry in the wilderness . . . and
I saw the Lord and he spake unto me saying
Joseph my son thy sins are forgiven thee. Go
thy way walk in my statutes and keep my commandments behold I am the Lord of glory."

He adds, in words presaging Lehi's, "my soul was filled with love and for many days I could rejoice with great Joy and the Lord was with me."[10] What the restoration represents, in perhaps its most essential dimension, was the reaffirmation, the facilitating and encouraging, of this personal knowledge of Christ and subsequent witness of his love to the widest possible audience. As the Lord would reveal this pattern, "It shall come to pass that *every soul* who forsaketh his sins and cometh unto me, and calleth on my name, and obeyeth my voice, and keepeth my commandments, shall see my face and know that I am" (D&C 93:1).

For a sixth–century Israelite, of course, much more is at stake in such a claim than the personal fulfillment of a beatific vision. The destiny of Nephi's entire people rests on the faithfulness with which they maintain

Christ as the center of their personal commitment and tribal devotion. And so a second principal reason for Nephi's frequent invocations of Isaiah is to encourage confidence in God's covenantal promises, preaching belief in Christ as the most essential precondition for their fulfillment. In a particularly powerful sermon, Nephi quotes Jacob teaching that Israel's "recovery," or gathering, will, in fact, depend upon "the day . . . when they shall believe in him." Then will "the Lord God fulfill his covenants" (2 Ne. 6:12–14).

Nephi adds his testimony and asserts to his people—with no chance of misunderstanding—that the Mosaic covenant has one purpose: "proving unto my people the coming of Christ" (2 Ne. 11:4). The Catholic theologian Stephen Webb paid Latter-day Saints the highest of compliments when he titled an article "Mormons Obsessed with Christ."[11] He had in mind Nephi's testimony in 2 Nephi 25 when making that judgment. There, Nephi affirms that his whole life and labor as a recordkeeper is to be a witness of Christ, hoping that by worshipping the Messiah, his people may find themselves faithful to the covenant and thereby secure the promises foretold by Isaiah. "For we labor diligently to write, to persuade our children, and also our brethren, to believe in Christ. . . . And we talk of Christ, we rejoice in Christ, we preach of Christ, we prophesy of Christ, and we write according to our prophecies, that our children may know to what source they may look for a remission of their sins" (verses 23, 26).

PART IV

More Plain and Precious Things

IV

More Plain and Precious Things

In the context of the two principal purposes of Nephi's second book—explicating the covenant and affirming Jesus as Christ—several points of theological clarity and correction emerge. In what follows, I will address five of them: the fall as fortunate, the principal of opposition, teachings on atonement, the centrality of agency, and the doctrine of Christ.

felix culpa, or the fortunate fall
Before Joseph Smith's contributions to religious understanding, the Christian version of covenant theology was rooted in the belief that God's intentions for mankind failed and his plan required a new formulation and new relationship to redeem us. "God's purpose and goal in redemption," writes one historian of religion, "is to reverse the sin, corruption and death introduced into humanity by Adam."[1]

Eden, in this almost universal understanding, is the setting for a catastrophe. Christian theology begins with the claim that something went terribly wrong in Eden. St. Augustine, the most formative voice in Christianity after Paul, writes, "Our first parents fell into open disobedience because already they were secretly corrupted; for the evil act had never been done had not an evil will preceded it."[2] For John Milton, whose poem about the fall was probably more widely read than the Bible, their fateful "treason" against an "incensed Deitie" is responsible for "all our woe" and "makes guiltie all [their] sons."[3] Jonathan Edwards expresses horror at human rebellion against a "holiness that was infinitely beyond human standards," making the attempt "infinitely evil."[4] If such views are true, then indeed, God's first plan—or covenant—was a failure, and a new one was needed. This, as we saw above, is the premise behind Christian covenant theology: the covenant made with Eve and Adam was broken, and so Christ comes thousands of years later to rectify the disaster.

Nephi quotes his father to the effect that such an understanding is utterly wrong. Turning almost two millennia of Christian understanding on its head, his words that Joseph Smith translates in 1829 pronounce the absolute necessity behind our first parents' decision: "And now, behold, if Adam had not transgressed he would not have fallen, but he would have remained in the garden of Eden. And all things which were created must have remained in the same state in which they were after they were created; . . . and they would have had no children; wherefore they would have remained in a state of innocence, having no joy, for they knew no misery; doing no good, for they knew no sin" (2 Ne. 2:22–29).

Here was a doctrine of the "fall" to radically distinguish the Church of Jesus Christ from the teachings of other Christian churches. Brigham Young and other readers of the Book of Mormon noted the scriptural volume's general congruence with biblical teachings, but this passage was a striking exception to the way Christians had been reading the Bible since Augustine. This doctrine, the understanding that Eve and Adam's transgression was a foreordained sacrifice in obedience to a higher law, ☞ is the only—or certainly the only conspicuous—Book of Mormon teaching that is emphatically at odds with the Bible as interpreted by millions of readers for millennia. What is astonishing is how slow Latter–day Saints themselves were to see the revolutionary implications of this reversal. Not surprisingly, perhaps, it was the women of the Church who first recognized this reading that made Eve a courageous heroine rather than a guilty culprit in human history. A writer for the *Woman's Exponent*, an independent Latter–day Saint newspaper, proposes this view as serious theology, but not until 1874, noting that "our great maternal progenitor is entitled to reverent honor for braving the peril that brought earth's children from the dark valley of ignorance and stagnation, and placed them on the broad, progressive plain, where they, knowing good and evil, joy and sorrow, may become as Gods. . . . Mother Eve, for taking the initiative in this advance movement, should receive encomiums of praise."[5]

As if to reemphasize Lehi's important work of destroying the legacy of seeing Eve and Adam as primeval villains in the human saga, the Book of Moses, which emerged so closely on the heels of the Book of Mormon, repeated the principle via Eve's psalm of joy: "Were it not for our transgression we never should have had seed, and never should have known good and evil, and the joy of our redemption, and the eternal life which God giveth unto all the obedient" (Moses 5:11).

As Elder John A. Widtsoe teaches, "Sometimes two possibilities are good; neither is evil. Usually however one is of greater import than the other. When in doubt each must choose that which concerns the good of others—the greater law—rather than that which chiefly benefits ourselves—the lesser law. . . . That was the choice made in Eden." *Evidences and Reconciliations* (Salt Lake City: Bookcraft, 1947), 2:78. Or as Joseph Smith preaches, God "foreordained the fall of man." "Discourse, 5 February 1840, as reported by Matthew L. Davis," *The Joseph Smith Papers*, Documents, ed. Matthew C. Godfrey, Spencer W. McBride, Alex D. Smith, and Christopher James Blythe, vol. 7, *September 1839–January 1841*, ed. Ronald K. Esplin, Matthew J. Grow, and Matthew C. Godfrey (Salt Lake City: Church Historian's Press, 2018), 176.

"Adam fell," in Lehi's eloquently economical phrase, "that men might be" (2 Ne. 2:25).

"And men are," Lehi continues, "that they might have joy." Joy, the end and purpose of human existence, involves several preconditions. Lehi is here entering into deep waters, articulating some of the foundational principles on which human thriving depends. In Lehi's view, God aspires to create a universe teeming with possibility, change, development, and variety. The God of Genesis, whose entire creative vocation consists of differentiation and variegation, is emphatically the same God recognized by Lehi. God purposes to foster a universe—and a human realm—that is rich in diversity, difference, and alternatives and that also teems with growth, novelty, and change. While classical and medieval minds imagined a God—and a universe—of static perfection, stasis in Lehi's conceiving is synonymous with sameness, stagnation, death, and purposelessness. He is remarkably explicit on this point: If Eve and Adam had not chosen to immerse themselves in a world of experiential, open-ended possibilities, then "all things which were created must have remained in the same state in which they were" (2 Ne. 2:22). Growth, flourishing, and human joy all require the vibrancy of a free soul choosing among numerous options. *This* is the meaning of the so-oft misquoted scripture "it must needs be, that there is an opposition in all things" (verse 11). Opposition here means not adversity but contrasts, alternatives in the nature of opposites, that are the very basis of all value. A near contemporary of Joseph Smith, the poet and mystic William Blake, made a similar point: "Without contraries is no progression."[6] Joseph Smith himself expressed this principal in similar language: "by proving contrarreties [*sic*], truth is made manifest."[7] To "prove," in nineteenth-century usage, is to ascertain or evaluate the truth or value of something by means of comparison or experiment.[8] In other words, no value emerges in a vacuum; meaning can only appear, truth can only reveal itself, by virtue of our experience of contrary aspects of reality.

A universe in which such sets of contraries are absent does not bear thinking about. As Lehi indicates (with a shudder):

"If not so, my first-born in the wilderness, righteousness could not be brought to pass, neither wickedness, neither holiness nor misery, neither good nor bad. Wherefore, all things must needs be a compound in one; wherefore, if it should be one body it must needs remain as dead, having no life neither death, nor corruption nor incorruption, happiness nor misery, neither sense nor insensibility. Wherefore, it must needs have been created for a thing of naught; wherefore there would have been no purpose in the end of its creation" (2 Ne. 2:11–12).

How utterly incredible that, for Lehi, the fate worse than death, the condition that he deplores as an unthinkable option, is perpetual innocence, or stasis. This revisionist account of Eden celebrates immersion in pain, difficulty, struggle, and variety of experience. The alternative would be "a compound in one" of "all things," a condition of "no life, neither death," meaningless sameness (2 Ne. 2:11). *That* is the condition for which "opposition" is the foil, the rescue. Lehi is quite explicit that our very status as beings with meaningful existence and capacity for action depends entirely upon such a scheme of opposition: "Wherefore, man could not act for himself save it should be that he was enticed by the one or the other" (verse 16).

We must find ourselves in a sphere of alternatives from which to choose; otherwise, there is no moral freedom. And without such agency, we would indeed be a "thing of naught" (2 Ne. 2:12). In a modern revelation, the Lord reaffirmed this teaching even more dramatically, "All truth is independent in that sphere in which God has placed it to act for itself, as all intelligence also; otherwise *there is no existence*" (D&C 93:30, emphasis added).

Only this restoration teaching gives full meaning to a biblical phrase that has confounded legions of commentators and theologians. It is subsequent to Eve and Adam's transgression, not their decision to remain in a world undifferentiated by the sweet and the bitter, that God recognizes, "behold, they have become as one of us" (Gen. 3:22). These baffling words have been dismissed as pure irony, divine sarcasm, or simple error. Presuming that God must be indignant at human aspirations to divine metamorphosis, the words have been read as indicating hot displeasure, not matter–of–fact recognition. In saying that he "has become as one of us . . . God was mocking Adam," explains the fourth–century theologian Ephrem the Syrian.[9] Centuries later, commentator Andrew Willet agrees that the Lord "derides their folly," "speak[ing] ironically." Reformers Phillip Melanchton, Peter Vermigli, and Konrad Pellikan all employ the term "irony" as well to explain away the plain meaning of the text.[10] Chrysostom went even further and simply denied the accuracy of the passage, since it is obvious, he writes, that "they did not become god" *or* "receive the knowledge of good and evil."[11] Lehi's teachings, however, make sense of the words as simple fact. Only by knowing—that is, by experiencing, being immersed in, and confronting good and evil— can we exist as independent agents, acting for ourselves and not simply being acted upon. Life in a variegated universe and the possession of the capacity to choose among alternatives are the prerogatives of divinity. No wonder Eve and Adam rejoiced in the recognition of what their choice in Eden made possible.

teachings on atonement

The great mystic Julian of Norwich, seeing a vision of the suffering Christ, contemplated not just his pain, but the pain of those who were witness to his agonies. "For ever the higher, the mightier, the sweeter that love be," she remarks, "the more sorrow . . . to see that body in pain that is loved." In that shared suffering, she continues, "Saw I a great oneing betwixt Christ and us."[12]

The beauty and power of Julian's language is in its recapture of the original meaning of a word now altered by overuse, misuse, and abuse: *atonement*. A little background on the term will return us to a meaning that the Book of Mormon affirms as its primary signification. Working in the fourteenth century, the Englishman John Wycliffe was determined that every boy at the plow should be able to read the Bible in his native tongue. Coming to Romans chapter 5, he came to the culminating work of Jesus Christ's sacrifice, which he expresses in this language: "we glory in God by our Lord Jesus Christ, by whom we have received now reconciling."[13] The gift of Christ, in his language, is reconciliation to God, a coming to complete harmony and unity in love and forgiveness. This was the sum total of Jesus Christ's great work effected in Gethsemane and on the cross. It was a few centuries later that William Tyndale would lose his life as a consequence of his efforts to render a more accurate translation by working with Greek and Hebrew originals. Sometime in the 1520s, he rendered Romans 5:11 this way: "we also joy in God by the means of our Lord Jesus Christ by whom we have received the atonement."[14]

There, in language reminiscent of Julian of Norwich, he emphasized the final consequence of Christ's sacrifice: *oneing*, or employing a recent English coinage, "at–one–ing," reconciling tantamount to joyful union with God. Words evolve and new meanings supplant the old. In the broader Christian tradition, *atonement* came fairly quickly to signify the payment of a debt, suffering or pain undergone to rectify a past wrong, and compensation or restitution. These ideas have become part of the theological heritage of a concept central to Christian understanding. However, it would be tragic if the mechanism by which atonement is carried out were to displace the effect it was meant to achieve. The word *atonement* should *not* serve primarily as a description of heroic sacrifice—but as description of the product, the outcome, of that sacrifice. *Atonement* is not a legal term referencing reparation or ransom or payment for sin, but, as Julian's related term suggests, it is ontological—that is, it refers to a mode of being that the sacrifice is meant to accomplish. As Julian imagines the words of Jesus, "I shall together gather you, and make you mild and meek, clean and holy, by *oneing* to me."[15]

Nephi is the first in the Book of Mormon to employ the term *atonement*, and he will use it more than any other writer until we get to Alma. It is so entirely fitting that in the very first chapter of this book of 2 Nephi, as Lehi bids farewell to his posterity, he bears witness to the fruits of the *oneing* that he himself has personally experienced: "I have beheld his glory, and I am encircled about continually in the arms of his love" (2 Ne. 1:15). One of the principal beauties—and instructive motifs—found in the Book of Mormon is the intensely personal, experiential testimonies that constitute the bulk of the latter. Unlike the great cosmic drama with which Genesis opens—where we are immersed into an infinite chaos being organized into star systems, terrestrial formations of land and sea, and human origins—the Book of Mormon opens with the particular, the local, and the autobiographical: "I, Nephi." And it is the personal encounter with Jesus that forms the silken thread leading from Lehi's eloquent testimony through those of Nephi and Jacob, then Enos, and on through to the brother of Jared and Moroni, who affirms so movingly, "then shall ye know that I have seen Jesus, and that he hath talked with me face to face" (Ether 12:39). An unparalleled virtue of the Book of Mormon is its forceful challenge to us to make our knowledge of Christ and his atonement personal and experiential rather than abstract and theoretical. The stories of Book of Mormon characters are filled with these individual encounters with the Divine. Prayer acquires an efficacy seldom seen in the Bible—and so does revelation. One scholar writes that in the Bible, "prophecy was preeminently the privilege of the prophets,"[16] and Abraham Heschel calls prophecy the "exegesis of existence from a divine perspective."[17] In the Book of Mormon, by conspicuous contrast, revelation is a gift available to all. A vision is granted to a young Nephi desirous of knowing for himself the vision seen by Lehi. Visions are also granted to wayward youths with hungering souls, to fathers worried about missionary sons, to believers curious about the nature of the spirit world, and to generals seeking to defend their people.

More specifically, however, the Book of Mormon invites us to experience personally the healing power of Christ. Significantly, this encounter is described with the same word that Wycliffe would use in his translation: three times, all in 2 Nephi, we are urged to be "reconciled," that is, made at one, with God (2 Ne. 10:24, 25:23, 33:9). These echoes containing the earliest meaning of the word *atonement* seem a beautifully divine restoration of a plain and precious truth. Christ has fulfilled his efforts to be at one with us. They include, as Nephi chronicled, a life of exemplary goodness; a suffering borne of solidarity in which he fully shared in "the pains of all men, yea, the pain of every living creature, both men, women, and children, who belong to the family of Adam" and a willing sacrifice of self on the cross (2 Ne. 9:21). It now remains for us to do our own work of "oneing" through "at-one-ing," or "reconciling" our wills to God.

The Book of Mormon's great power is in its proven capacity to convince readers to taste of the fruit of the tree—which represents the Love of God—for themselves. The prophetic emphasis of the book's writers is to "seek this Jesus," in Moroni's words (Ether 12:41). Presumably, becoming "at one" with Christ should be our emphasis as well. One irony of the Bible is that although Christ's atoning sacrifice and the at-one-ing effect are the foundation of our faith, the fact that "the New Testament does not offer a unified account of the atonement of Jesus Christ is a theological commonplace," as one scholar notes.[18] In this regard, the Book of Mormon—and 2 Nephi—are particularly valuable.

The first point Lehi makes about the atonement is that Christ's death and resurrection make possible our own conquest of death. His principal purpose was to "bring to pass the resurrection of the dead," so that we may again "stand in the presence of [God]" (2 Ne. 2:8). Nephi adds his testimony that the coming Messiah will "suffer . . . the pains of every living creature . . . that the resurrection might pass upon all men" (2 Ne. 9:21–22). Before any question of judgment, eternal rewards, or punishments, before any discussion of salvation or its preconditions, there is the brute fact of death. And Lehi recognizes that this first gift of resurrection, universal and unearned, is an unconditional promise that we will live again. In the history of religious conflict—and in the lives of questing disciples—the fine print seems to get all the attention. The wars of the Reformation era and the fires of the Inquisition were fueled by disputes over the nature of the Trinity, the degree of God's presence in the Eucharist, the question of whether sacraments are symbols or channels of grace, and so forth. In our lives, we may so anguish over the minutia of worship forms or doctrinal minutia that we commit the sin of ingratitude for the most unfathomably remarkable gift of all. As one Latter–day Saint with more sense than certainty wrote, "It seems a pity to take one's immortality for granted, to expect it and count on it. It seems a pity to be so sheltered from the terror of death that one's gratitude for the resurrection is merely dutiful and perfunctory. Perhaps truly there are religious advantages to doubt. Perhaps only a doubter can appreciate the miracle of life without end."[19]

Jacob, even more than Lehi, marvels at the gift of a universal resurrection, actually breaking into ecstatic praise. As Nephi quotes him,

O the wisdom of God, his mercy and grace! For behold, if the flesh should rise no more our spirits must become subject to that angel who fell from before the presence of the Eternal God, and became the devil, to rise no more. O how great the goodness of our God, who prepareth a way for our escape from the grasp of this awful monster; yea, that monster, death and hell. . . . And because of the way of deliverance of our God, the Holy One of Israel, this death, of which I have spoken, which is the temporal, shall deliver up its dead; which death is the grave. Wherefore, death and hell must deliver up their dead, . . . and it is by the power of the resurrection of the Holy One of Israel. . . . O how great the plan of our God! (2 Ne. 9:8–13).

The atonement addresses sin as well as death; but—as we might expect in a text that was not filtered through a traditional Christian lens—abundant life, not forgiveness, is the focus. Throughout the Book of Mormon we find a version of the gospel that is not presented via translations or traditions that dilute or misinterpret its original meaning. One such example is the absence of what the great theologian Krister Stendahl referred to as the unhealthy obsession with sin and depravity that crept into the early Christian church in the fourth century.

> The point where Paul's experience intersects with his . . . understanding of the faith, furthermore, is not 'sin' with its correlate 'forgiveness.' It is rather when Paul speaks about his weakness that we feel his deeply personal pain. Once more we find something surprisingly different from the Christian language that most of us take for granted: it seems that Paul never felt guilt in the face of this weakness—pain, yes, but not guilt. It is not in the drama of the saving of Paul the sinner, but it is in the drama of Paul's coming to grips with what he calls his 'weakness' that we find the most experiential level of Paul's theology.[20]

Christianity's fixation on the "plagued conscience" is a development that Stendahl traces to Augustine three centuries after Paul and then to the Reformers over a thousand years later. In the early Christian church, the emphasis was on the Christ's conquest of death—and it is that conquest that both Lehi and Jacob highlight in their teachings on atonement.

This gift that both Lehi and Jacob associate with "the merits, and mercy, and grace of the Holy Messiah," is that he gives his life "that he may bring to pass the resurrection from the dead" (2 Ne. 2:8). And because of this "intercession for all," we will all once again "stand in the presence of him" (verse 10). The sense in which they understood Christ to be their Redeemer had that primary meaning. "They are redeemed from the fall," that is, redeemed from the temporal death that followed Eve and Adam's choice in the garden, not from any imagined sin that we inherit (verse 26).

Jacob takes this lesson to heart and passes it on in his own sermon in chapter 9. Because of this "infinite atonement," this "corruption" puts on "incorruption" (verse 7). Otherwise, our flesh would "rise no more" but "become subject to that angel who fell" (verse 8). And again, because of the resurrection's "deliverance," "death and hell must deliver up their dead . . . and the bodies and spirits of men will be restored one to the other" (verse 12). The pains which Christ suffers are suffered so "that the resurrection might pass upon all men" (verse 22).

Of course, this conquest of death entails more than biological regeneration. The atonement, in contemporary Latter-day Saint thought, has been appropriated to solve the two most profound problems of human existence: (1) the specter of physical death and (2) the trauma of sin, woundedness, and alienation from God. Nephi suggests that while Christ's sacrifice solves these two dilemmas, they are separate and, thus, are separately addressed in his suffering and death. As Jacob teaches in chapter 10, God will "raise [us] from death by the power of the resurrection." In addition, he will "raise [us] . . . also from *everlasting death* by the power of the atonement" (verse 25, emphasis added). What this seems to indicate is that rising from the grave will represent Christ's (and our) triumph over death. Our rebirth in Christ, which we covenant to undertake now, represents a more significant triumph over that death we are all subject to until we live in Christ. That rebirth is signified by our baptism and commemorated every sacrament service. Among the first Christians, Ignatius called the Lord's Supper "the medicine of immortality," the first ordinance in our "divinization or deification."[21] In the primitive Church, converts were often baptized in large groups at Easter since the significance of both Easter and one's baptism was birth to a new life, partaking of divinity.[22]

How, exactly, does Christ's death work in us or upon us to bring about that second effect of his sacrifice: actual at–one–ing, or reconciling, our birth into a new life in Christ? How does his suffering alleviate our own? And how can this transpire without sacrificing our own agency and responsibility? The book of 2 Nephi sheds some light on such questions, though our understanding is augmented by other Book of Mormon writers, too.

At its roots, Christ's suffering on the cross is usually connected with the notion of satisfying the demands of justice (2 Ne. 9:26; Alma 42:15, etc.). However, the Book of Mormon suggests that we have misunderstood what "justice" means. For Book of Mormon prophets, justice is neither some unimpeachable cosmic universal nor the inflexible standard of a legalistic heavenly monarch. It is, rather, another name for what, from a human perspective, is simply the honoring of human choice. Genuine moral agency must entail genuine consequences. Choice must be choice of something. In John Stuart Mills's classic treatment, human liberty requires the freedom "of doing as we like, *subject to such consequences as may follow*" (emphasis added).[23] If choice is to be more than an empty gesture of the will, more than a mere pantomime of decision–making, there must be some guarantee that any given choice will eventuate in the natural consequences connected with that choice.

This appears to be the meaning of Lehi in his sermon on freedom when he says, "the law is given to men," and as a result, they are "free forever, . . . to act for themselves and not to be acted upon, save it be by the punishment of the law" (2 Ne. 2:5, 26). The relationship between choice and consequence is made clear through those laws or principles that Christ himself articulates: "Wherefore, the ends of the law [are those] the Holy One hath given, unto the inflicting of the punishment which is affixed . . . to answer the ends of the atonement" (verse 10). So consequences are established and a "punishment . . . is affixed . . . in opposition to that of the happiness which is affixed" (verses 11, 10). Simply circumventing those consequences—out of mercy or any other motive—would not only abrogate human agency but eliminate the very distinctions that make possible a universe of meaningful differences and, thus, meaningful existence.

What kind of freedom would there be if no real consequence attached to any deliberate choice? What we experience as punishment is, from another perspective, the simple and natural consequence of choices that reconcile us to or alienate us from each other and from the light of Christ—"that which gives life to all things" (see D&C 88:13). God does not inflict pain or punishment. He forewarns us of the sorrows that follow in the wake of agency wrongly employed. Judgment, in this conception, entails the recognition that we inherit the condition we have chosen, hence, "we shall have a perfect knowledge of all our guilt, and . . . the righteous shall have a perfect knowledge of their enjoyment" (2 Ne. 9:14).

One crucial, essential caveat is the following: we never make choices with a perfect fulness of understanding or with agency that is perfectly untainted by circumstance, ignorance, genetic impairments, bodily limitations, and so on. Yet the consequences of such a compromised exercise of agency can ripple out through generations in ways we could never imagine nor ever be able to repair. And since we generally do not choose with a fullness of understanding, a will that is uncontaminated, or an intention that is fully deliberate, these acts cannot be considered fully intentional. How could we then be held fully accountable for the pain we cause or the alienation we suffer? For we do not, in the fullest sense of the word, choose these repercussions.

Because our agency is seldom perfect and undiluted, Christ can intercede on our behalf without violating our agency; he can take upon himself the consequences of our poor choices, because as Alma$_2$ will explain, "repentance could not come unto men except there were a punishment" (Alma 42:16). But his assumption of those pains can only displace our own without violating our agency if we demonstrate through a change of heart—and of behavior—that we are determined to choose differently now and in the future. In that case, and only in that case, as we "repent . . . believe . . . and endure . . . the mercies of the Holy One of Israel have claim upon [us]" (2 Ne. 9:24–25). In this view of atonement, our ultimate choices are validated and honored. "One [must be] raised to happiness according to his desires of happiness, or good according to his desires of good; and the other to evil according to his desires of evil" (Alma 41:5).

agency

A restoration view of agency and God's determination to honor it from the foundations of the world is crucial to understanding how the principle of atonement operates. The Book of Mormon clarifies the reality of moral freedom and its significance in the life of discipleship. One astute observer notes the "almost obsessive Mormon concern for free moral agency."[24] The restoration occurred at the very moment when Christianity was rediscovering—or at least reasserting—the role of human freedom of choice in the saga of salvation. Augustine, the virtual founder of Catholicism, and the Reformers Luther and Calvin had all denied freedom of the will. "I, indeed, labored in defense of the free choice of the human will," Augustine explains, "but the grace of God conquered."[25] For Luther, "God foresees nothing contingently, but that He both foresees, determines, and actually does all things, by His unchangeable, eternal, and infallible will. By this thunderbolt the whole idea of free–will is smitten down and ground to powder."[26] As for Calvin, he professed belief in a free will, but it was without substance; we are free to act, he holds, but only according to our nature. And since even infants bring from the womb a nature that is "odious and abominable to God," we are powerless to choose salvation.[27]

Arminius, the Dutch theologian credited with leading a successful revolt against the dominion of determinism and predestination in Christian thought, was only slightly more inclined toward freedom. He writes,

"the Free Will of man towards the True Good is not only wounded, maimed, infirm, bent, and weakened; but it is also imprisoned, destroyed, and lost: And its powers are not only debilitated and useless unless they be assisted by grace."[28]

With the rise of Methodism, whose founder, John Wesley, was influenced by Arminius, a shift in religious culture was underway. A growing emphasis on the role of individual choice and self–determination was central to America's cultural development at this time as well and was reinforced by the larger European currents of the age, known as Romanticism. The Book of Mormon lends scriptural support to these cultural and religious developments.

Nephi in particular, quoting Lehi, writes the most ringing endorsement of human agency to be found in any scriptural record:

> And the Messiah cometh in the fulness of time, that he may redeem the children of men from the fall. And because that they are redeemed from the fall they have become free forever, knowing good from evil; to act for themselves and not to be acted upon, save it be by the punishment of the law at the great and last day, according to the commandments which God hath given. Wherefore, men are free according to the flesh; and all things are given them which are expedient unto man. And they are free to choose. (2 Ne. 2:26–27)

"The doctrine of human depravity is denied," notes one surprised pamphleteer of the era in responding to the Book of Mormon. "Total depravity is denounced. Children are said . . . [to] have no sin, and are alive in Christ."[29] Another critic protests that if, as the Book of Mormon taught, "atonement was made for the original transgression of the whole human race, . . . then every human being since that event must be born into the world like a sheet of paper; and you may write good or bad upon it as you please."[30]

A perfectly blank sheet of paper may be a slight exaggeration as an analogy for the condition of the human soul at birth; however, it is closer to the truth than the version of inherited sin and corrupt nature common in the religious discourse of Joseph Smith's day. The Book of Mormon, while celebrating the freedom with which Christ gifts us, does not consider such freedom absolute. We are free, Lehi teaches, insofar as we are rescued from the bondage of death, redeemed from Satan's dominion over the dead. "Redeemed from the fall they have become free forever" (2 Ne. 2:26). Such freedom is qualified, however, presuming that people "are instructed sufficiently that they know good from evil" (2 Ne. 2:5), "have . . . the law given to them" (2 Ne. 9:26), are not blinded by the inheritance of "wicked and abominable traditions" (Hel. 15:7), or "wounded" by the corruption of the scriptural record.[31] "To act for [our-] selves and not to be acted upon" (2 Ne. 2:26), to *choose* to reconcile our will to God's, is the possibility that Christ's gracious atonement reaffirms.

This emphasis on human freedom and agency is therefore central to Lehi's conception of the gospel covenant. And in this regard, the principle of opposition as the precondition for meaningful existence that we saw above may be the key. Choice, to be meaningful, must be a choice of something. Joy, which Lehi positioned as the very purpose of our existence, can only come as a consequence of choosing joy—or the path and conditions conducive to it. And here we see the link between atonement as resurrection and atonement as that which guarantees our agency. It does this in two ways. First, it makes possible our immersion in a world of alternatives and opportunities without incurring the everlasting consequences of choices made in the infancy of our spiritual development. We "taste the bitter, that [we] may know to prize the good" (Moses 6:55). But we do not remain in that condition of alienation from God; we do not need to suffer the eternal bitterness of choices made along our path toward godliness. The restoration recuperates this original Christian understanding that the fall was necessary— the atonement is the provision for the collateral damage we experience and inflict along the path of spiritual education. As the early church father Irenaeus wisely taught,

> Wherefore also he drove him out of Paradise,
> and removed him far from the tree of life, not

because he envied him the tree of life, as some
venture to assert, but because he pitied him,
[and did not desire] that he should continue
a sinner for ever, nor that the sin which sur–
rounded him should be immortal, and evil
interminable and irremediable. But he set
a bound to his [state of] sin, by interposing
death, and thus causing sin to cease . . . so that
man, ceasing at length to live to sin, and dying
to it, might begin to live in God.[32]

Second, the resurrection we enjoy as a meritless
gift places us once again in the presence of God to
experience the fruits of those choices that moved us
toward reconciliation with God. We again "stand in the
presence of him to be judged of him according to the
truth and holiness which is in him," in Lehi's words
(2 Ne. 2:10). And that judgment, he continues, is according to the choices we made in a world where there was
"opposition in all things" (2 Ne. 2:11), that is, the array of
manifold enticements on which we choose to place our
affections and, thus, choose our own destinies. Jacob
makes the same connection. Christ's "infinite atonement" brings us from "this first death unto life," where
our eternal condition becomes a simple extenuation
of the life we chose amidst all the options: "they who
are righteous shall be righteous still, and they who are
filthy shall be filthy still" (2 Ne. 9:15–16). It could hardly
be clearer: the atonement—by overcoming death and
preserving agency—allows us to persist eternally as
those beings we have chosen to be.

doctrine of Christ

The purpose of the restoration, as we have seen, was a
repair of the new and everlasting covenant, and Jesus
Christ is the pivotal figure in that covenant. If a correct

understanding of Jesus Christ and his mission had been current in 1820, the Lord would have had no need to call a prophet to bring about a restoration. The loss of the "plain and precious things" so lamented by Nephi must have included, at the very least, the true "doctrine of Christ" (2 Ne. 31:2, 21). And this doctrine of Christ must be intimately related to the covenant with which Nephi devoted himself to explicating and teaching.

In Joseph Smith's view, which was shaped by the Book of Mormon, the apostasy was largely a matter of "plain and precious things" that were taken away, leaving our world without an understanding of the origins and designs associated with the everlasting covenant. First and foremost, as Nephi clearly teaches, is the fact that there is one covenant—an eternal covenant—that incorporates the entire human family within the scope of Christ's healing and salvific power, not two separate and distinct covenants (old and new). This unity of the covenant paved the way for Joseph Smith's fuller restoration of the everlasting covenant that transpired in the years after he translated the Book of Mormon, which brought about a correct understanding of (1) the background, purpose, and extent of the covenant and (2) premortal origins, mortal incarnation, and eventual theosis and sealing into eternal families, fully achieved through temple covenants that constitute chains of belonging, completing our journey from intelligence to deity.

In this context, the apostasy did not consist of overly pessimistic accounts of human depravity and a universal fall, but of losing sight of the fall itself as a necessary and premeditated immersion of humankind into the crucible of experience, suffering, and schooling in the practice of love. Apostasy was not so much about baptizing at the wrong age or in the wrong medium. It was about not knowing that baptism makes us—all of us eventually—literally of Christ's family and his coheirs. It was not about simple difference in standards of sexual practice or marriage's purpose per se. It was about failing to see marriage as a key mode of eternal association, associations that are at the very heart of what heaven is. Finally, an apostasy did not mean that God had ceased to grace individuals with inspiration, guidance, and truth. In fact, some of the inspiration that came to individuals in those centuries before the restoration, from what God called those "holy men [and women] that ye know not of" (D&C 49:8), provided illumination that Joseph Smith would eventually prophetically gather into the fulness of the restoration. In sum, "restoration" was not about correcting particular doctrines or practices as much as it was about restoring their cosmic context. Only in this larger context, with God's designs restored, can we understand what Nephi calls "the doctrine of Christ," including its major elements of baptism, repentance, and feasting on the word.

baptism

After indicating his general topic of "the doctrine of Christ," the first principle to which Nephi turns, in words of "plainness," is to "be baptized in the name of [the] beloved Son" (2 Ne. 31:2, 11). How are we to understand this sacrament, and what is its central meaning? First, it is imperative to note that baptism is always associated with Christ's name. We are baptized "in his name" (2 Ne. 9:23). What does that mean? Partaking of the sacrament in weekly worship, we recommit to "take his name upon us." King Benjamin does not mention baptism, but he does teach the same principle of adoption to those who embrace a covenantal relationship to the Savior. He tells his people that in taking the name of Christ upon themselves, they have made a "covenant" to "be called the children of Christ, his sons, and his daughters" (Mosiah 5:7).

Paul explicitly gives this process its correct name of adoption. Baptism is the ordinance of adoption into God's family, with Christ having "spiritually begotten" us (Mosiah 5:7). During the Mosaic phase of the everlasting covenant, circumcision reminded the Jewish people that certain covenantal obligations and privileges were theirs by birth (Romans 3:1–2). Baptism replaces circumcision as a rite more appropriately symbolic of adoption available to all, not just to one designated people. As Paul explains, baptism signifies the death of our old identity and our rebirth with a new one. We become, via "the Spirit of adoption," "children, . . . joint-heirs with Christ" (Rom. 8:16–17). Hence, one is baptized as a sign of one's desire and decision to be adopted into God's heavenly family. As Joseph Smith teaches, one must "subscribe [to] the articles of adoption to enter . . . the kingdom of God."[31] Baptism is the first formal ordinance that sets in motion our incorporation into this new kind of relationship to Heavenly Parents, to Christ as our personal Healer and Redeemer from death, and to a larger community of brothers and sisters. The question that here arises is, are we not already God's spirit children? Why then do we need adoption?

While we do not inherit original sin or come with any primeval guilt attached to us, we all make choices from early in life that emanate from a nature that is human—we are biologically, culturally, and socially conditioned to seek our own will rather than God's. Recognizing the reality of our spiritual separation from our Heavenly Parents as a consequence of the veil (occasioned by mortal birth and compounded by personal sin), adoption became for the first generations of Saints a reincorporation into a binding and eternal relationship, an ordinance signifying what the Book of Mormon refers to as our reconciliation to the will of God rather than the will of the flesh (2 Ne. 10:24). According to the apostle Parley P. Pratt, following the "alienation of our race from God," we have "lost all claim" to be heirs. That is why we must be spiritually reborn, and receive "the spirit of adoption whereby [we] can cry, Abba, Father."[34] As Pratt writes in the *Millennial Star*, God's purpose is "to bring us back from that state of alienation into his own family."[35] Repairing our "state of alienation," we can recross "the very threshold of his house, . . . having a legal claim, by the laws of heaven, on the privileges of sonship [and daughtership]."[36] The influential Orson Spencer writes that adoption by baptism remedies our condition of "rebellion against the laws of Christ."[37] B. H. Roberts reaffirms this seeming paradox: "It is chiefly through adoption, through obedience to the Gospel of Christ, that man in the scripture is spoken of as being a son [or a daughter] of God." At the same time, humans are literally "by nature the [children] of God," and human destiny portends an eventual, full likeness to God. But that process, given human alienation from God through personal sin, requires spiritual rebirth, and hence "adoption" into the heavenly kingdom, and into sonship (or daughtership) with God.[38]

The direct tie between the new and everlasting covenant, which envisions just this process, and baptism as the first mortal step we make in that direction is made explicit in the 1830 revelation cited above. Baptism, those words of God state, "*is* a new and an everlasting covenant, even that which was from the beginning" (D&C 22:1; emphasis added). Employing the same phrasing as 2 Nephi, the same revelation then refers to baptism as the "gate" by which we "enter in" (verse 4; see 2 Ne. 31:9). The exact "Order & Ordinances of the Kingdom were instituted by the Priesthood in the council of Heaven before the World was," taught Joseph Smith, and this understanding of baptism—an ordinance that affirms a covenant "which was from the beginning"—is a key element of a restoration of what had been lost to Christian understanding.[39]

Nephi also explicitly refers to baptism as the act that brings about our adoption when he says, we "take upon [us] the name of Christ by baptism" (2 Ne. 31:13; cf. Moroni 4, 5). Hence, the first ordinance of the gospel—baptism—is in effect an ordinance of formal adoption by Christ, which is brought about by covenant. In one of their very rare doctrinal expositions, the First Presidency in 1916 explained that the "sense in which Jesus Christ is regarded as the 'Father' has reference to the relationship between Him and those who accept His gospel and thereby become heirs of eternal life."[40] It is this particular covenant, so foundational to everything else that transpires in our spiritual journey home, that we reaffirm weekly. In renewing our pledge to "take upon [us] the name of [the] Son" (Moro. 4:3) we are reminded that we have assumed a new identity—or have been more fully restored to our identity that unites us to a heavenly family.

Doctrine and Covenants 22:1 thus constitutes the most emphatic statement that baptism in Latter-day Saint theology is the first formal and effectual step toward integration of the individual into the new and everlasting covenant, a step that will make one the seed of Abraham, and by extension, a literal child of Heavenly Parents in the celestial family order. Lacking that particular covenantal context and understanding, "although a man should be baptized an hundred times it availeth him nothing" (D&C 22:2). Baptism's covenantal significance—which transcends its status as a sign and vehicle of personal cleansing—is the defining meaning of the ordinance. This leaves us with a second question: is baptism not "for remission of sins" (Article of Faith 4)?

The death of our old self and adoption as a child of Christ are inseparably connected with a remission of sins. If baptism is to signify our adoption by Christ, if it is the "gate by which we enter" into a new relationship and a new life (2 Ne. 31:9), then in order to take upon us this new identity, we must be shorn of the old. Obtaining a remission of sins, or an erasure of the old self, is so that we *may begin a new life in Christ as his children*. It may, in fact, be in an attempt to capture the tandem nature of these two functions, new birth and remission of sin, that Nephi refers to baptism by water as the entrance to the gate and the associated baptism by fire as the remission of sin. In his words, "For the gate by which ye should enter is repentance and baptism by water; and then cometh a remission of your sins by fire and by the Holy Ghost" (2 Ne. 31:17).

repentance

It is no coincidence that the literal translation of *metanoeo*, which is usually rendered "to repent," is "mind–change." For the Greeks, the mind, or *nous*, was the faculty of judgment and the location of the will. Even if we know of this equivalence between repenting and having a change of mind (or heart), we may not fathom the full implications this has for our own discipleship. We generally think of repentance as forsaking sin, having devastating sorrow for our own hurtful action. In the King James Version of the Bible, the expression "broken heart" appears only once, in the thirty–fourth psalm ("The Lord is nigh unto them that are of a broken heart; and saveth such as be of a contrite spirit"; verse 18). The New Testament writers do not pick up the expression, but Lehi, who was familiar with the brass plates, did. The effects of Christ's sacrificial offering, are extended to those "who have a broken heart and a contrite spirit," Nephi records him as saying (2 Ne. 2:7).

For Nephi, however, this theme of brokenness seems to suggest a vulnerability, or openness to reshaping and reforming, that is central to a disciple's life. In his magnificent psalm, he prayerfully attests that his own "heart is broken and [his] spirit . . . contrite" (2 Ne. 4:32). But vastly more is at play here in reshaping the will than simply forsaking sin. In Nephi's psalm, he does not just lament his shortcomings; he yearns for the same assurance of God's embrace that his father knew, to be "encircle[d] . . . around in the robe of [God's] righteousness" just as his father was "encircled . . . in the arms of [God's] love" (verse 33; 2 Ne. 1:15).

In subsequent chapters, Nephi more directly links repentance to the positive work of educating the will to love and aspire to higher and nobler ends. His emphasis is on the joyful prospect of the Christ–centered life, not an unhealthy preoccupation with guilt and byways of the past. For Nephi, this heart–change heralds a "baptism of fire," "the tongue of angels," "shout[ing] praises," "a perfect brightness of hope," and spiritual "feast[ing]" on Christ's words (2 Ne. 31:13–19). For Alma$_2$, it involves letting all "the affections of thy heart be placed upon the Lord forever" (Alma 37:36).

Inhabiting a mortal body, we find ourselves oriented around biological needs and drives, environmental pressures, worldly values, and aspirations. To be adopted into Christ's family, we have to shift our frame of reference, redirect our affections, and shatter the paradigms and patterns that have encased us in the confining attire of atomistic individualism and material preoccupations. Latter–day Saints committed to a belief in human "whole[ness] from the foundation of the world" (Moses 6:54) should particularly resonate with one of the Hebrew terms for repent, shub. It signifies, in the words of one biblical scholar, "a turning away from present things and returning to the point of departure."[41]

Repentance, in the limited sense of forsaking sin, is far too narrow a term to encompass this full range of reorientation and transformation suggested by the word's Hebrew and Greek counterparts. As the Epistle to the Romans indicates, the challenge is to engage in a "renewing of your mind," meaning the *whole* mind (Rom. 12:2). For Nephi, too, baptism launches a process rather than completes one. As he writes, "after ye have gotten into this strait and narrow path, I would ask if all is done? Behold, I say unto you, nay" (2 Ne. 31:19). Reeducating the heart, as the seat of our desires, is the lifelong project to which we commit ourselves at baptism.

feasting on the word

Twice Nephi associates a commitment to a life of discipleship with "feasting upon the word of Christ" (2 Ne. 31:20, 32:3). Feasting is more than reading. To feast is to partake of in a spirit of gladness and joy. But feasting may imply a good deal more. To ingest a food is to assimilate it and transform it into something useful for the individual. This seems to be what Nephi urges in his repeated practice of likening the scriptures to his people and circumstances. Regardless of who Isaiah had in mind as his original audience or context, his words "may be likened unto you," Jacob tells the Nephites (2 Ne. 6:5).

What we may have missed is that when Nephi performs his acts of scriptural appropriation to the situation at hand, he is participating in a practice that completely pervades the Book of Mormon. The dynamic, vibrant life of scripture—as something that is generated, assimilated, transformed, and transmitted in endless ways and in ever new contexts—finds its most dramatic instance with a repentant sinner, Alma the Elder, well into the subsequent narrative. Coming from a heathen people far removed from the righteous Nephites, Alma$_1$ begins, surprisingly, to preach Christ to his peers: "And now it came to pass that Alma, who had fled from the servants of King Noah, repented of his sins and iniquities, and . . . began to teach . . . concerning that which was to come, and also concerning the resurrection of the dead, and the redemption of the people, which was to be brought to pass through the power, and sufferings, and death of Christ" (Mosiah 18:1–2).

How did Alma$_1$ obtain knowledge of Christ? He heard the preaching of Abinadi, an itinerant prophet martyred by the wicked Noah. And Alma$_1$ "did write all the words which Abinadi had spoken" (Mosiah 17:4). Where did Abinadi, who appears suddenly in the narrative with no background or introduction, get his knowledge? In chapters 13 and 14 of Mosiah, we see him reading the words of Moses and of Isaiah to Noah's court, finding in them clear foreshadowing of a "God [who should] himself . . . come down among the children of men, and . . . redeem his people" (18:1). Where did Abinadi obtain those scriptures? He was a member of Zeniff's colony, which was an offshoot of the major Nephite settlement, and apparently, they took copies of the Nephite records with them when they departed Zarahemla and resettled Lehi–Nephi. And those Nephite records? As we already learned early in the Book of Mormon, Nephi and his brothers absconded with Laban's brass plates, which contained the writings of Moses, Isaiah, and several other Hebrew prophets. So we have a clear line of transmission from prophetic utterance, to brass plates, to Nephi's small plates, to Zeniff's copy, to Abinadi's gloss, to Alma$_1$'s transcription. And that is only half the story. From Alma$_1$, we learn that those teachings become a part of his written record. When he and his band of exiles arrive back in the major colony of Zarahemla, King Mosiah reads to the assembled people "the account of Alma and his brethren" (25:6). King Mosiah, as guardian of the large plates, presumably incorporates the record into his own record. Those plates are subsequently abridged by Mormon, the late fourth–century Nephite editor. In every instance, the scriptures provide doctrine, inspiration, or guidance for a group or individual far removed from the last audience who consumed them.

It is in Nephi, however, that we find the most explicit modeling of how we are to liken scripture to ourselves. It has long been pointed out that Nephi practices a kind of approach to scripture that is similar to the Jewish practice of *midrash*. Midrash derives from a Hebrew root that signifies "to inquire, investigate." Its "major characteristic," according to one authority, "is its attempt to make a biblical text contemporary and relevant."[42] With words that seem strikingly pertinent to Nephi's practice, one scholar thinks that the essence of midrash is to be found in its "feeding of the life–impulse when harassed and threatened by life circumstances."[43]

Nephi invokes Isaiah repeatedly, not just to affirm his prophecies concerning the destiny of Israel and of future events but to adapt Isaiah's words to his people's particular predicament. Latter–day Saint scholars have already shown how he thoroughly infuses his prophecies of Nephite destiny with passages from Isaiah, repurposing them to fit a people and place Isaiah may never have had in mind.[44] But Nephi's role as prophet to his people does not entirely overshadow his personal discipleship and the strength he finds in seeing scriptural history as a template and inspiration for his private journey. In many places, but especially in his most poignant literary effusion, the famous psalm of Nephi, his recurrent allusions to the travails of Moses and the children of Israel strike home in a personal way: in spite of the murmurings and trials of hostile brothers and recalcitrant followers, he knows that "God hath been my support; he hath led me through mine afflictions in the wilderness." He can attest that Christ "manifesteth himself unto all those who believe in him by the power of the Holy Ghost" (2 Ne. 26:13) because that promise had already been fulfilled in his life. "He hath filled me with his love, even unto the consuming of my flesh" (2 Ne. 4:20–21). And he finds that he has the power to make Isaiah's words about scripture speaking out of the dust factually true in reference to himself. That discovery may be the most remarkable exemplification of what it means to liken scripture unto ourselves. His language was clear in this regard: "I will liken his words unto my people," he writes (2 Ne. 11:2). Knowing God has "made the sea [his] path," he considers that his people are effectively "upon an isle of the sea" (2 Ne. 10:20). And knowing that God "remember[s] those who are upon the isles of the sea," he assures himself and his people that they are not forgotten (2 Ne. 29:7). Trusting that "all things which have been given of God from the beginning of the world . . . are the typifying of [Christ]" (2 Ne. 11:4), he finds scriptural evidence of him everywhere. As God gave Moses power "to heal the nations," and bring forth water to a thirsty people, so does he trust that "Jesus Christ" will come, "whereby man can be saved" (2 Ne. 25:20). Did reading Isaiah's references to "the words of a book" to come forth from "them which have slumbered" add energy to his own record–keeping activity (2 Ne. 27:6)?

So we are to feast on the words of Christ, but with a pattern clearly intended. We find in the scriptures our personal path to Christ. Nephi, a sojourner in a strange land, found Christ in the brass plates, learning that "all things which have been given of God from the beginning of the world, unto man, are the typifying of him" (2 Ne. 11:4). Alma₁, a young man in a corrupt kingdom, found him in the scriptures quoted by Abinadi, learning of his "power, and sufferings, and death" (Mosiah 18:2). The Mulekites, having "brought no record with them," are only able to rediscover Christ when united to a people who "look forward unto the Messiah" and make that hope a central theme of their scriptural record (Omni 1:17; Jarom 1:11). But we do not find Christ by learning how others found him. Only when we make the scriptures speak to us, finding our place in God's story, does the past Atoner for sin or future Redeemer of Israel become our present Hope and Healer.

In the verses with which Nephi concludes his second book, he bears his final witness of Jesus Christ. In a particularly revealing plea, he urges his readers that even if they "believe not in these words," may they at least "believe in Christ" (2 Ne. 33:10). It is a pure-hearted desire. More important than vindicating ourselves, our faith, or our own understanding of the gospel is the greater task to which we are called: to direct others, by word or deed, to Christ the Healer.

Endnotes

SERIES INTRODUCTION

1. Elder Neal A. Maxwell, "The Children of Christ," Devotional Address, Brigham Young University, 4 February 1990, https://speeches.byu.edu/talks/neal-a-maxwell_children-christ/ (accessed 16 April 2019).

2. Elder Neal A. Maxwell, "The Inexhaustible Gospel," Devotional Address, Brigham Young University, 18 August 1992, https://speeches.byu.edu/talks/neal-a-maxwell/inexhaustible-gospel/ (accessed 6 August 2019).

3. Elder Neal A. Maxwell, "The Book of Mormon: A Great Answer to 'The Great Question,'" Book of Mormon Symposium Address, Brigham Young University, 10 October 1986, reprinted in *The Voice of My Servants: Apostolic Messages on Teaching, Learning, and Scripture,* eds. Scott C. Esplin and Richard Neitzel Holzapfel (Provo, UT: Religious Studies Center, Brigham Young University; Salt Lake City: Deseret Book, 2010), 221–38, https://rsc.byu.edu/archived/voice-my-servants/book-mormon-great-answer-great-question (accessed 16 April 2019).

INTRODUCTION

1. Hilary Brueck, "NASA Wants to Send Humans to Mars in the 2030s—Here's the Step-by-Step Timeline," *Business Insider*, March 1, 2018, https://www.businessinsider.com/when-will-we-colonize-mars-nasa-timeline-2030s-2018-2 (accessed 20 February 2020).

2. Jon Levenson, *Sinai and Zion: An Entry into the Jewish Bible* (San Francisco: HarperSanFrancisco, 1985), 181.

3. Levenson, Sinai and Zion, 122–23.

4. Worried that his men might lose heart in the face of "the great power and fierceness of the Aztec nation," the Spanish conquistador Hernán Cortés scuttled his small army's ships, precluding any return to Spain. Winston A. Reynolds, "The Burning Ships of Hernán Cortés," *Hispania* 24, no. 3 (September 1959): 318.

5. Risa Levitt Kohn, *A New Heart and a New Soul: Ezekiel, the Exile, and the Torah* (London: Sheffield, 2002), 1.

6. George Robinson, *Essential Torah: A Guide to the Five Books of Moses* (New York: Schocken Books, 2006), 120.

7. John Romer, *Testament: The Bible and History* (New York: Henry Holt, 1988), 107.

8. Cited in Kohn, *A New Heart*, 110.

9. Alexander Fantalkin and Oren Tal, "The Canonization of the Pentateuch: When and Why? Part II." *Zeitschrift für die Alttestamentliche Wissenschaft* 124: 202–3.

10. Kaufmann Kohler et al., "Covenant," *Jewish Encyclopedia*, 1906, http://www.jewishencyclopedia.com/articles/4714-covenant (accessed 20 February 2020).

I

1. Levi Richards Journal, cited in Dean C. Jessee, "The Earliest Documented Accounts of Joseph Smith's First Vision," in *Opening the Heavens: Accounts of Divine Manifestations 1820–1844*, ed. John W. Welch (Provo and Salt Lake City: Brigham Young University Press and Deseret, 2005), 24.

2. Wilford Woodruff, Journal, 28 November 1841. Church History Library.

3. Ehat and Cook, *Words of Joseph Smith*, 87–88.

4. Ehat and Cook, *Words of Joseph Smith*, 41.

5. "Ordinances were instituted in heaven before the foundation of the world." Joseph Smith mentions baptism in particular as a foreordained sacrament of salvation. So was confirmation with its associated sign of the dove. Ehat and Cook, *Words of Joseph Smith*, 210, 159–60.

6. Ehat and Cook, *Words of Joseph Smith*, 210, 254.

7. Joseph Smith only exempted sons of perdition from this covenantal promise. Ehat and Cook, *Words of Joseph Smith*, 353.

8. *The Song of the Pearl*, trans. Han J. W. Drijvers, Robert M. Grant, Bentley Layton, and Willis Barnstone, in *The Gnostic Bible*, ed. Willis Barnstone and Marvin Meyer (Boston: Shambhala, 2003), 388–94. A typical reading of the poem sees it as recounting "the soul's bodily incarnation and its eventual disengagement from the body." Bentley Layton, *The Gnostic Scriptures: A New Translation with Annotations and Introductions* (Garden City, NY: Doubleday, 1987), 366.

9. Joseph Jacobs and Judah David Einstein, "Palestine, Holiness of," *Jewish Encyclopedia*, 1906, http://www.jewishencyclopedia.com/articles/11867–palestine–holiness–of (accessed 20 February 2020).

10. The Presbyterian Church stated this version of "supersession theology" in repudiating it in 1987. Quoted in R. Kendall Soulen, *The God of Israel and Christian Theology* (Minneapolis: Fortress Press, 1996), 3.

11. Ebenezer Henderson, revising Charles Buck's views in 1833, saw the Mosaic covenant as recapitulating the Adamic version. Charles Buck and Dr. Henderson, "Covenant," in *Theological Dictionary* (London: James Duncan, 1833), 259.

12. Robert Davidson, "Covenant," in *The Oxford Companion to Christian Thought*, ed. Adrian Hastings (Oxford: Oxford Unversity Press, 2000), 142.

13. Joseph Wilhelm, "Mediator (Christ as Mediator)," in *The Catholic Encyclopedia*, vol. 10 (New York: Robert Appleton, 1911), http://www.newadvent.org/cathen/10118a.htm (accessed 20 February 2020).

14. Grant Hardy, "The Book of Mormon and the Bible," in *Americanist Approaches to* The Book of Mormon, ed. Elizabeth Fenton and Jared Hickman (New York: Oxford University Press, 2019), 109.

15. Kohler et al., "Covenant."

16. Levenson, *Sinai and Zion*, 41.

II

1. Levenson, *Sinai and Zion*, 179.

2. *The Complete Discourses of Brigham Young*, ed. Richard S. Van Wagoner (Salt Lake City: Smith–Petit Foundation, 2009), 2: 919.

3. Fred C. Collier and William S. Harwell, eds., *The Kirtland Council Minute Book* (Salt Lake City: Collier's, 2002), 34.

4. Ehat and Cook, *Words of Joseph Smith*, 110.

5. "To the Saints Abroad," *Elders' Journal of the Church of Latter Day Saints* 1, no. 4 (July 1838): 54.

6. Ehat and Cook, *Words of Joseph Smith*, 212.

III

1. Pratt, Miscellaneous Minutes, 242.

2. "Lectures on Faith," *Doctrine & Covenants*, 1835 ed., 19.

3. The sources are given in John A. Tvedtnes, "Jeremiah's Prophecies of Jesus Christ," in *The Most Correct Book* (Salt Lake City: Cornerstone, 1999), 101–2.

4. Eusebius, *The History of the Church from Christ to Constantine*, trans. G. A. Williamson (Middlesex, England: Dorset, 1983), 41.

5. John Tvedtnes, "The Messiah, the Book of Mormon, and the Dead Sea Scrolls," in *The Most Correct Book*, 343. Tvedtnes cites examples from scrolls 11Q13, 4Q246, and 4Q521 (328–43).

6. Margaret Barker, *The Great Angel: A Study of Israel's Second God* (Louisville: John Knox, 1992), 2. See also her *The Older Testament: The Survival of Themes from the Ancient Royal Cult in Sectarian Judaism and Early Christianity* (London: SPCK, 1987).

7. Daniel Boyarin, *The Jewish Gospels* (New York: New Press, 2012), 72–73.

8. Shirley Lucass, *The Concept of Messiah in the Scriptures of Judaism and Christianity* (London: Bloomsbury, 2011), 13–14.

9. J. F. C. Harrison, *The Second Coming: Popular Millenarianism*, 1780–1850 (New Brunswick, NJ: Rutgers University Press, 1979), 191, cited in Gordon S. Wood, "Evangelical America and Early Mormonism," *New York History* 61 (October 1980): 380.

10. "History, circa Summer 1832," in *The Joseph Smith Papers*, Histories, ed. Karen Lynn Davidson, David J. Whittaker, Mark Ashurst-McGee, and Richard L. Jensen, vol. 1, *Joseph Smith Histories, 1832–1844*, ed. Dean C. Jessee, Ronald K. Esplin, and Richard Lyman Bushman (Salt Lake City: Church Historian's Press, 2012), 5.

11. Stephen Webb, "Mormons Obsessed with Christ," *First Things*, February 2012, https://www.firstthings.com/article/2012/02/mormonism-obsessed-with-christ (accessed 20 February 2020).

IV

1. Roger E. Olson, *The Story of Christian Theology* (Downers Grove, IL: InterVarsity Press, 1999), 277.

2. St. Augustine, *City of God*, trans. Marcus Dods (North Charleston, SC: Createspace, 2015), 314.

3. John Milton, *Paradise Lost*, bk. 3, lines 207, 187, 290; bk. 1, line 3. Ed. A. W. Verity (London: Cambridge University Press, 1924), 79, 78, 82, 9.

4. George M. Marsden, *Jonathan Edwards: A Life* (New Haven, CT: Yale University Press, 2003), 112.

5. S. M. K. [Sarah M. Kimball], "Plea for the Women of Massachusetts and Mother Eve, vs. Kate Bowers," *Woman's Exponent 2*, no. 18 (February 15, 1874): 141, cited in Boyd J. Petersen, "'Redeemed from the Curse Place Upon Her': Dialogic Discourse on Eve in the *Women's Exponent*," *Journal of Mormon History* 40, no. 1 (Winter 2014): 155–56.

6. William Blake, "The Marriage of Heaven and Hell," *Complete Poetry and Selected Prose of John Donne and the Complete Poetry of William Blake* (New York: Random House, 1941), 651.

7. "Letter to Israel Daniel Rupp, 5 June 1844," p. 1, *The Joseph Smith Papers*, https://www.josephsmithpapers.org/paper-summary/letter-to-israel-daniel-rupp-5-june-1844/1 (accessed 20 February 2020).

8. Noah Webster, *An American Dictionary of the English Language* (New York: S. Converse, 1828), s.v. "prove."

9. Andrew Louth, ed., *Ancient Christian Commentary on Scripture: Genesis 1–11* (Downers Grove, IL: InterVarsity, 2001), 1:100.

10. The glosses of Willet, Melanchton, Vermigli, and Pellikan are all found in John L. Thompson, ed., *Reformation Commentary on Scripture: Genesis 1–11* (Downers Grove, IL: InterVarsity, 2012), 1:177.

11. Chrysostom, *Homilies on Genesis 7*, cited in Louth, *Ancient Christian Commentary*, 1:101.

12. Julian of Norwich, *Revelations of Divine Love* (London: Methuen, 1901), 40. I have modernized the spelling.

13. Rom. 5:11 in *Wycliffe Bible* (Cranbrook, British Columbia: Praotes, 2009), 748.

14. William Tyndale, cited in appendix 1 in *Early Modern Communi(cati)ons: Studies in Early Modern English and Culture*, ed. Kinga Földváry and Erzsébet Stróbl (Newcastle, England: Cambridge Scholars Publishing, 2012), 304.

15. Julian, *Revelations*, 59.

16. "Prophecy," in F. L. Cross and E. A. Livingstone, eds., *Oxford Dictionary of the Christian Church* (Oxford: Oxford University Press, 1997), 1336;

17. Abraham Heschel, *The Prophets* (New York: Harper and Row, 1962), xviii.

18. Ryan W. Davis, "The Authority of God and the Meaning of the Atonement," *Religious Studies* 50, no. 4 (December 2014): 406.

19. Levi S. Peterson, "A Christian by Yearning," *The Wilderness of Faith* (Salt Lake City: Signature, 1991), 134.

20. Krister Stendahl, *Paul among the Jews and Gentiles* (Philadelphia: Fortress, 1979), 40–41, 85.

21. Olson, *Story of Christian Theology*, 48.

22. See Marcellino D'Ambrosio, *Who Were the Church Fathers?: From Clement of Rome to Gregory the Great* (London: SPCK, 2015), 14.

23. John Stuart Mill, *On Liberty*, 2nd ed. (Boston: Ticknor and Fields, 1863), 28.

24. Sterling McMurrin, *The Theological Foundations of the Mormon Religion* (Salt Lake City: University of Utah Press, 1965), 52.

25. Augustine, *Retractions*, trans. Mary Inez Bogan (Washington, DC: Catholic University of America Press, 1968), 120.

26. Augustine, *De Servo Arbitrio*, in *The Ideas of the Fall and of Original Sin*, trans. Norman Powell Williams (London: Longmans, Green, 1927), 434.

27. John Calvin, *Institutes of the Christian Religion*, trans. Henry Beveridge (Peabody, MA: Hendrickson, 2008), 153.

28. Jacob Arminius, *The Works of Arminius*, 3 vols., trans. James Nichols and William Nichols (Grand Rapids, MI: Baker Book House, 1991), 3:192.

29. Samuel Haining, *Mormonism Weighed in the Balances of the Sanctuary, and Found Wanting* (Douglas, Isle of Man: Robert Fargher, 1840), 31.

30. R. Clarke, *Mormonism Unmasked, or, the Latter-day Saints in a Fix* (London: Banks, 1849), 7–8.

31. 1 Nephi 13:32 (1830 edition).

32. Irenaeus, *Against Heresies* III.xxxiii.6, cited in Alexander Roberts and James Donaldson, eds., *The Ante-Nicene Fathers* (Grand Rapids, MI: Eerdmans, 1977), 1:457.

33. Ehat and Cook, *Words of Joseph Smith*, 256.

34. [Parley P. Pratt?], "Law of Adoption," *Millennial Star* 4, no. 2 (June 1843): 17 and "Editorial," *Millennial Star* 4, no. 2 (June 1843): 31.

35. Parley P. Pratt, "Of Future Punishments," *Millennial Star* 3, no. 2 (March 1843): 181.

36. Pratt, "Law of Adoption," 18.

37. Orson Spencer, *Letters Exhibiting the Most Prominent Doctrines of the Church of Jesus Christ of Latter-day Saints* (Liverpool, England: self-pub., 1848), 56.

38. B. H. Roberts, *The Mormon Doctrine of Deity* (Salt Lake City: Deseret News, 1903), 165.

39. Ehat and Cook, *Words of Joseph Smith*, 215.

40. The First Presidency and Quorum of the Twelve, "The Father and the Son," *Improvement Era* 19, no. 10 (August 1916), 936.

41. W. L. Holladay, *The Root Shub in the OT* (1958), cited in Horst Balz and Gerhard Schneider, eds., *Exegetical Dictionary of the New Testament* (Grand Rapids, MI: Eerdmans, 1981), 2:416.

42. Renee Bloch, cited in Gary G. Porton, "Midrash," in *The Anchor Bible Dictionary*, ed. David Noel Freedman (New York: Doubleday, 1992), 4:818.

43. H. Slonimsky, "The Philosophy Implicit in the Midrash," *Hebrew Union College Annual* 27 (1956): 235–90, cited in Gary G. Porton, "Midrash," in *The Anchor Bible Dictionary*, ed. David Noel Freedman (New York: Doubleday, 1992), 4:818.

44. See Heather Hardy and Grant Hardy, "How Nephi Shapes His Readers' Perceptions of Isaiah," in *Reading Nephi Reading Isaiah: Reading 2 Nephi 26–27*, ed. Joseph M. Spencer and Jenny Webb (Salem, OR: Salt Press, 2011), 37–62. For a more extensive treatment, see Joseph M. Spencer, *The Vision of All: Twenty-Five Lectures on Isaiah in Nephi's Record* (Salt Lake City: Kofford Books, 2016).

Editions of the
Book of Mormon

Most Latter-day Saints are familiar principally with the official edition of the Book of Mormon published in 2013 by the Church of Jesus Christ of Latter-day Saints. It contains the canonical text of the book, divided into chapters of relatively even length with numbered verses for ease of access. Its footnotes aim to assist readers in seeking doctrinal understanding.

Other Book of Mormon editions are available and often helpful. Among these are official editions from earlier in the scripture's publishing history, which are relatively accessible. There are also editions published recently by a variety of presses meant to make the text more readable. Both types of editions are referred to throughout *Book of Mormon: brief theological introductions*. Also of importance (and occasionally referred to) are the manuscript sources for the printed editions of the Book of Mormon.

manuscript sources

Unfortunately, the original manuscript of the Book of Mormon was damaged during the nineteenth century, but substantial portions of it remain. All known extant portions have been published in typescript in Royal Skousen, ed., *The Original Manuscript of the Book of Mormon: Typographical Facsimile of the Extant Text* (Provo, UT: FARMS, 2001). A future volume of the Joseph Smith Papers will publish images of the extant manuscript, along with a typescript.

After completing the original manuscript's dictation, Joseph Smith assigned Oliver Cowdery to produce a second manuscript copy of the text. That manuscript has been called the printer's manuscript since it was designed for use by the first printer of the Book of Mormon. The printer's manuscript, which is more or less entirely intact, also contains corrections and other editorial markings inserted when the second (1837) edition of the Book of Mormon was being prepared. A typescript of the printer's manuscript can be found in Royal Skousen, ed., *The Printer's Manuscript of the Book of Mormon: Typographical Facsimile of the Entire Text in Two Parts,* 2 vols. (Provo, UT: FARMS, 2001). Full color images of the manuscript were subsequently published along with a transcript in the Joseph Smith Papers series: Royal Skousen and Robin Scott Jensen, eds., *Printer's Manuscript of the Book of Mormon*, 2 vols., vol. 3 of the *Revelations and Translations* series of The Joseph Smith Papers, ed. Dean C. Jessee, Ronald K. Esplin, and Richard Lyman Bushman (Salt Lake City: Church Historian's Press, 2015). The images and transcript of the printer's manuscript are also available at the Joseph Smith Papers website (www.josephsmithpapers.org/the–papers/ revelations–and–translations/jsppr3).

historical editions

Multiple editions of the Book of Mormon were published during the lifetime of Joseph Smith. The first edition, published in Palmyra, New York, in 1830, appeared without versification and with fewer chapter divisions than the present canonical text. The text of the 1830 edition is available electronically at the Joseph Smith Papers website (www.josephsmithpapers.org/the–papers/revelations–and– translations/jsppr4) and in print through various publishers as a replica edition. The 1830 text is also available in Robert A. Rees and Eugene England, eds., *The Reader's Book of Mormon* (Salt Lake City: Signature Books, 2008), which is divided into seven pocket–sized volumes (each with an introduction by a scholar).

Joseph Smith introduced numerous minor changes into the text of the Book of Mormon when it was prepared for a second edition in 1837. Many of these changes are marked in the printer's manuscript. Most were aimed at correcting grammatical issues, but some, in a small handful of cases, were also aimed at clarifying the meaning of the text or its doctrinal implications. The 1837 edition is available electronically at the Joseph Smith Papers website (www. josephsmithpapers.org/the–papers/revelations–and–translations/ jsppr4).

A third edition was prepared under Joseph Smith's direction in 1840, and evidence makes clear that the original manuscript was consulted carefully in preparing this edition. Some important errors in the earlier editions were corrected, further grammatical improvements were introduced, and a few other changes were made to the text for purposes of clarification. The 1840 edition can be read at the Joseph Smith Papers website (www.josephsmithpapers.org /the–papers/revelations–and–translations/jsppr4). It forms the basis for at least one printed edition as well: *The Book of Mormon*, trans. Joseph Smith Jr. (New York: Penguin Books, 2008), which contains a

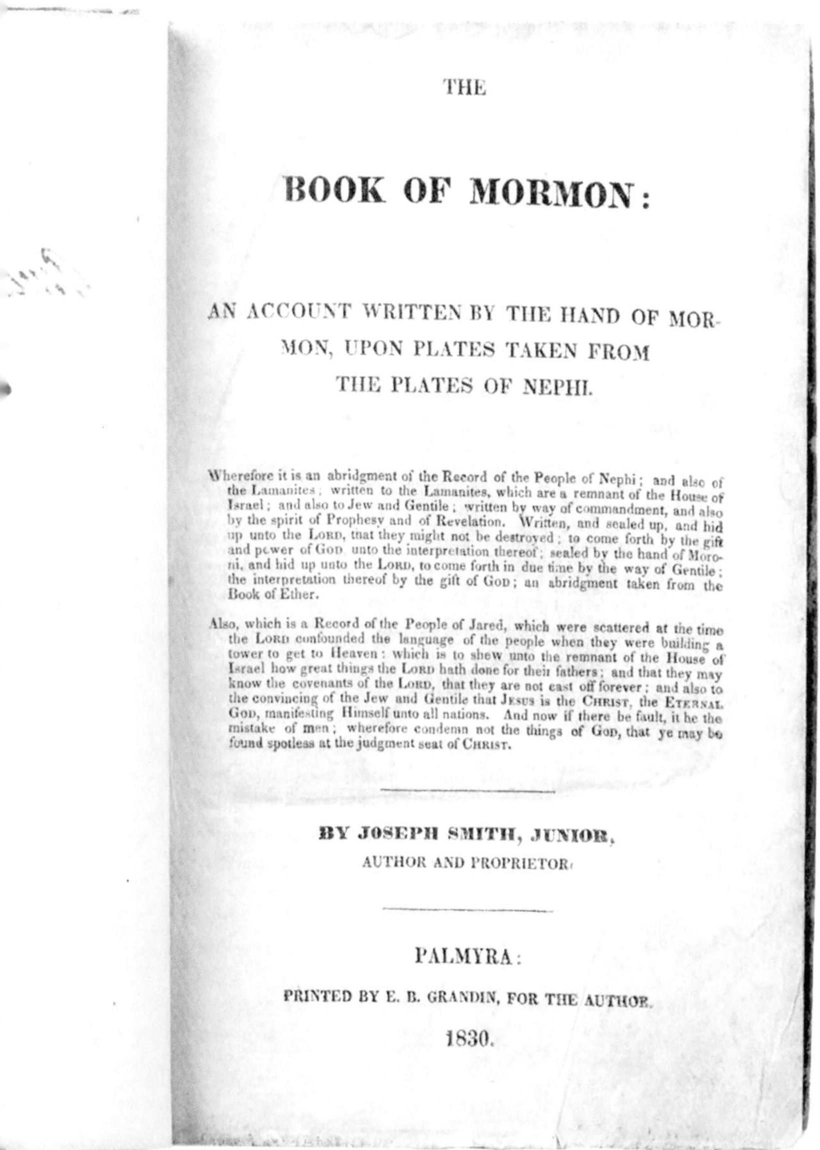

THE

BOOK OF MORMON:

AN ACCOUNT WRITTEN BY THE HAND OF MOR-
MON, UPON PLATES TAKEN FROM
THE PLATES OF NEPHI.

Wherefore it is an abridgment of the Record of the People of Nephi; and also of the Lamanites, written to the Lamanites, which are a remnant of the House of Israel; and also to Jew and Gentile; written by way of commandment, and also by the spirit of Prophesy and of Revelation. Written, and sealed up, and hid up unto the LORD, that they might not be destroyed; to come forth by the gift and power of GOD unto the interpretation thereof; sealed by the hand of Moroni, and hid up unto the LORD, to come forth in due time by the way of Gentile; the interpretation thereof by the gift of GOD; an abridgment taken from the Book of Ether.

Also, which is a Record of the People of Jared, which were scattered at the time the LORD confounded the language of the people when they were building a tower to get to Heaven: which is to shew unto the remnant of the House of Israel how great things the LORD hath done for their fathers; and that they may know the covenants of the LORD, that they are not cast off forever; and also to the convincing of the Jew and Gentile that JESUS is the CHRIST, the ETERNAL GOD, manifesting Himself unto all nations. And now if there be fault, it he the mistake of men; wherefore condemn not the things of GOD, that ye may be found spotless at the judgment seat of CHRIST.

BY JOSEPH SMITH, JUNIOR,

AUTHOR AND PROPRIETOR.

PALMYRA:

PRINTED BY E. B. GRANDIN, FOR THE AUTHOR.

1830.

FIGURE 2 The title page of the original 1830 edition of the Book of Mormon. © Intellectual Reserve, Inc.

helpful introduction by Laurie Maffly-Kipp, a scholar of American religious history.

One other edition of the Book of Mormon appeared during the lifetime of Joseph Smith—an 1841 British edition, which was largely based on the 1837 edition and therefore lacked corrections and other improvements that appear in the 1840 edition. It, too, is available electronically at the Joseph Smith Papers website (www.josephsmithpapers.org/the-papers/revelations-and-translations/jsppr4).

In 1879, Latter-day Saint apostle Orson Pratt completed one of the more influential editions of the Book of Mormon published after Joseph Smith's death. Pratt lamented that too many Latter-day Saints left the scripture unread on the shelf. He sought to create an easier reading experience by dividing up the originally long chapters and adding verse numbers—revisions which have largely remained unchanged in the Church's official edition to the present. He also pioneered a system of cross-references and other explanatory footnotes. Most of Pratt's notes were removed or replaced in subsequent official editions—most thoroughly in the Church's 1981 edition when new descriptive chapter headings were introduced. These headings can still be found, with a few minor updates, in the 2013 edition.

A detailed and helpful devotional treatment of the publication history of the Book of Mormon can be found in Richard E. Turley Jr. and William W. Slaughter, *How We Got the Book of Mormon* (Salt Lake City: Deseret Book, 2011). These authors trace developments in the format and study apparatuses used to present the text of the Book of Mormon to audiences from the 1850s to the present.

study and reading editions

The most important scholarly editions of the Book of Mormon are Grant Hardy, ed., *The Book of Mormon: A Reader's Edition* (Urbana and Chicago: University of Illinois Press, 2003); and Royal Skousen, ed., *The Book of Mormon: The Earliest Text* (New Haven, CT: Yale University Press, 2009).

Hardy's edition repackages the text of the 1921 public domain edition of the Book of Mormon. It contains a helpful introduction, a series of useful appendices, and a straightforward presentation of the text in a highly readable format. Footnotes are minimal—they are used only to clarify direct references or allusions within the text, to track dates, or to alert readers about original chapter divisions. This edition contains modern chapter and verse divisions, but they are unobtrusively typeset. The text is presented in straightforward paragraphs, with one-line headings marking text divisions. Poetry is set off in poetic lines, as in modern editions of the Bible.

Skousen's edition is the result of his quarter-century-long work with the manuscript and printed sources for the Book of Mormon text. The edition aims to reproduce as closely as can be reconstructed the words originally dictated by Joseph Smith to his scribes. Chapter and verse divisions familiar from recent editions are in the text (and symbols mark original chapter breaks), but the text is presented in what Skousen calls "sense lines"—each line containing (on Skousen's reconstruction) approximately what the prophet would have dictated at one time before pausing to allow his scribe to write. The edition contains helpful introductory material and a summary appendix noting significant differences between *The Earliest Text* and the current official edition. It is otherwise without any apparatus for the reader.

The most significant edition of the Book of Mormon deliberately constructed for a lay reading audience is Grant Hardy, ed., *The Book of Mormon: Another Testament of Jesus Christ, Maxwell Institute Study Edition* (Salt Lake City and Provo, UT: Neal A. Maxwell Institute, Deseret Book, and BYU Religious Studies Center, 2018). In this edition, Hardy uses the text of the 2013 official edition of the Book of Mormon but presents it in a readable way for everyday students of the volume. This edition reproduces the best of what appears in Hardy's *Reader's Edition* but adds further resources in the introductory and appendix materials. The footnotes are updated and expanded to include variant readings from the original and printer's manuscripts, and to provide notes about other textual details. The body of the text is presented, as in the *Reader's Edition*, in a straightforward fashion, readable and interrupted only by one-line headings. Modern chapter and verse divisions, as well as original chapter divisions, are easily visible.

Index

Colophon

The text of the book is typeset in Arnhem,
Fred Smeijer's 21st-century-take on late
18th-century Enlightenment-era letterforms
known for their sturdy legibility and clarity
of form. Captions and figures are typset in
Quaadraat Sans, also by Fred Smeijers.
The book title and chapter titles are typeset
in Thema by Nikola Djurek.

Printed on Domtar Lynx 74 gsm,
Forest Stewardship Council (FSC) Certified.

Printed by Brigham Young University Print & Mail Services

Woodcut illuminations **Brian Kershisnik**
Book design & typography **Douglas Thomas**

114

2 Nephi 4:5 behold, my sons and my daughters, I cannot go down to my grave save I should leave a blessing upon you